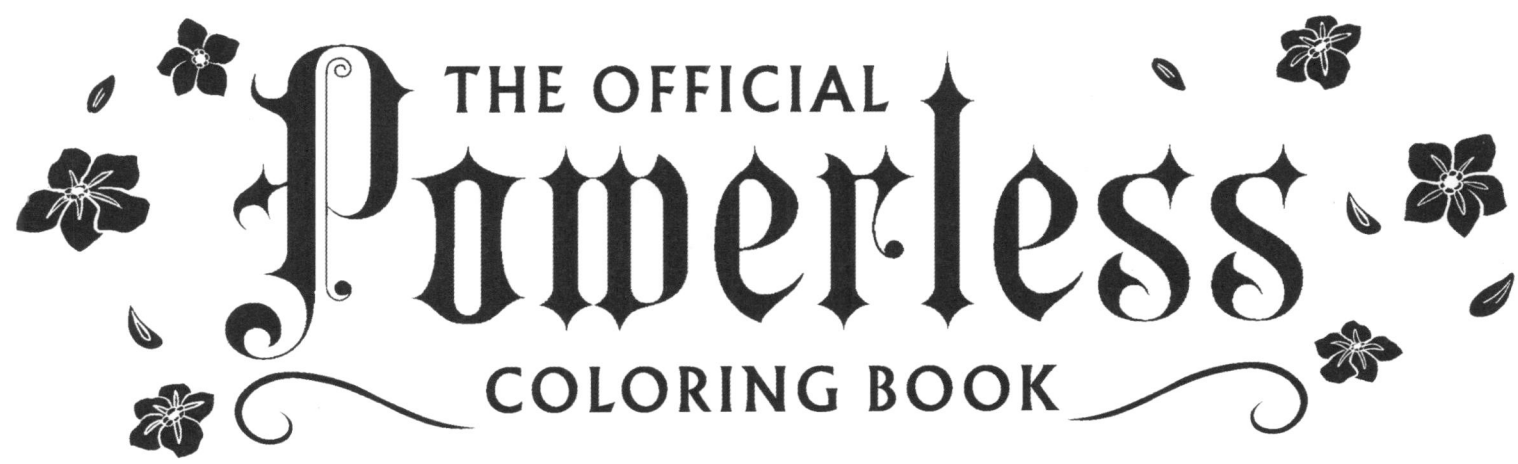

THE OFFICIAL Powerless COLORING BOOK

SIMON & SCHUSTER BFYR

An imprint of Simon & Schuster Children's Publishing Division

1230 Avenue of the Americas, New York, New York 10020

Text © 2023 by Lauren Roberts
POWERLESS™ is a trademark of Lauren's Library LLC
Illustration © 2026 by Alex Forrest
First published in Great Britain in 2026 by Simon & Schuster UK Ltd

For information about special discounts for bulk purchases, please contact Simon & Schuster Special Sales at 1-866-506-1949 or business@simonandschuster.com.

Simon & Schuster strongly believes in freedom of expression and stands against censorship in all its forms. For more information, visit BooksBelong.com.

The Simon & Schuster Speakers Bureau can bring authors to your live event. For more information or to book an event, contact the Simon & Schuster Speakers Bureau at 1-866-248-3049 or visit our website at www.simonspeakers.com.

The text for this book was set in Bembo Std.

The illustrations for this book were rendered digitally.

Printed and bound in Great Britain by Bell and Bain Ltd, Glasgow

First Edition

10 9 8 7 6 5 4 3 2 1

ISBN 9798347116867

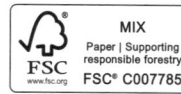
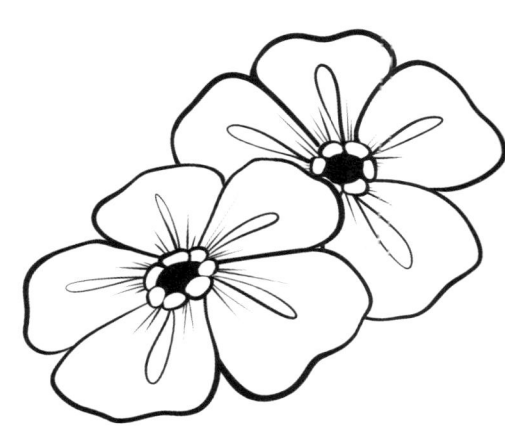

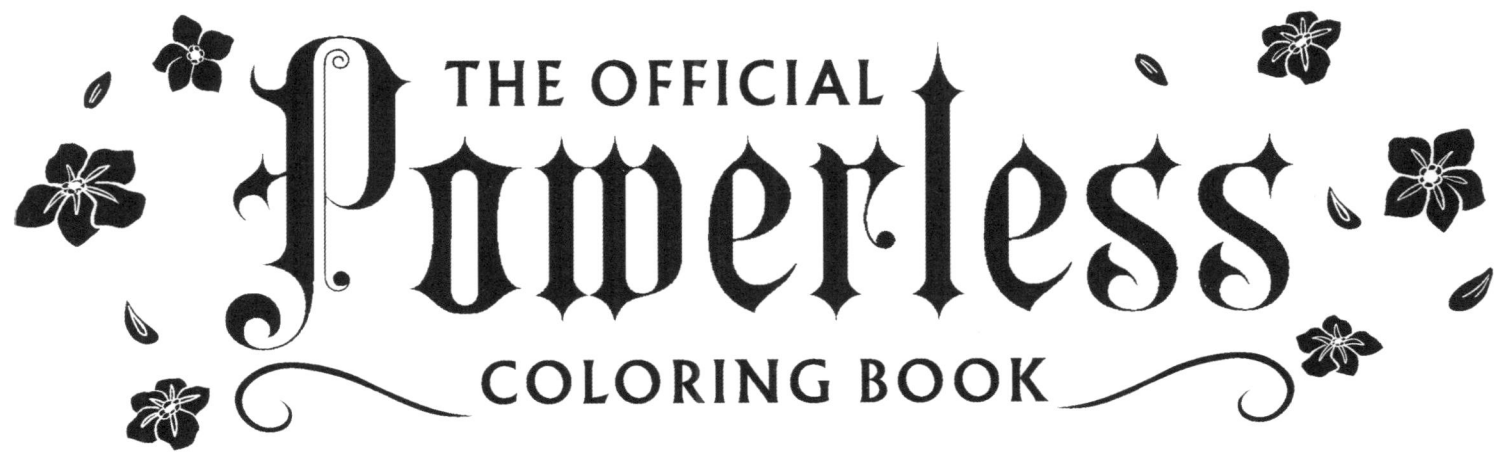

THE OFFICIAL Powerless COLORING BOOK

with illustrations by
ALEX FORREST

LAUREN ROBERTS

SIMON & SCHUSTER BFYR

NEW YORK • AMSTERDAM/ANTWERP • LONDON
TORONTO • SYDNEY/MELBOURNE • NEW DELHI

I sling my pack from my back and pull out the crumpled red silk from within, unable to suppress my smile as a look of awe settles on her face.

She greedily claws the silk from my hands, running her fingers through the soft folds of the fabric. Peeking up through the curly bangs hanging in her hazel eyes, she looks at me as though I've just single-handedly eradicated the Plague rather than stolen fabric from a woman not much better off than we are.

Like I'm the hero and not the villain.

Adena's smile could rival the sun over the Scorches Desert. "Pae, you and your sticky fingers work magic, you know that?"

She throws her arms around my neck, pulling me into a crushing embrace that causes more honey to ooze down my vest and pool in my pockets.

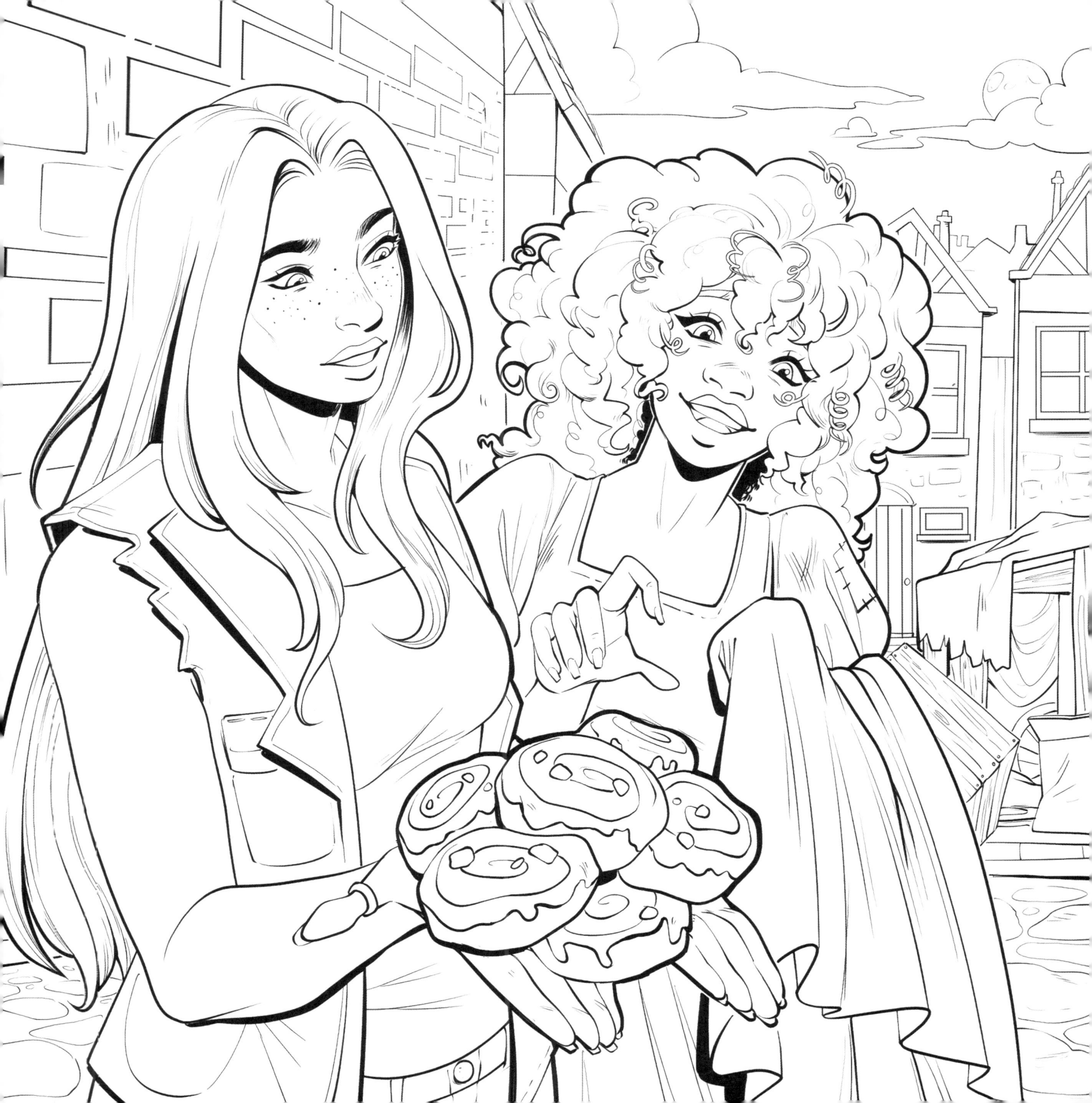

"See, isn't this fun?"

Kitt grits his teeth against my strike. "Riveting."

I fall into a familiar trance, letting my feet dance around the ring as we spar, getting lost in the rhythm. My mind clears. My body hums with energy. I've always felt most alive when I fight. It's what I was made to do, what has kept me sane over the years of training and tutoring.

"A dimwitted king is a dead king."

Father's words ring through my mind, having been drilled through my skull after every complaint about my tedious lessons as a boy. Though, I won't have to worry about being a dead or dimwitted king, seeing that I won't be a king at all. And after arguing just that to Father, he kindly created a new saying for me to live by.

"A dimwitted Enforcer is a defeated empire."

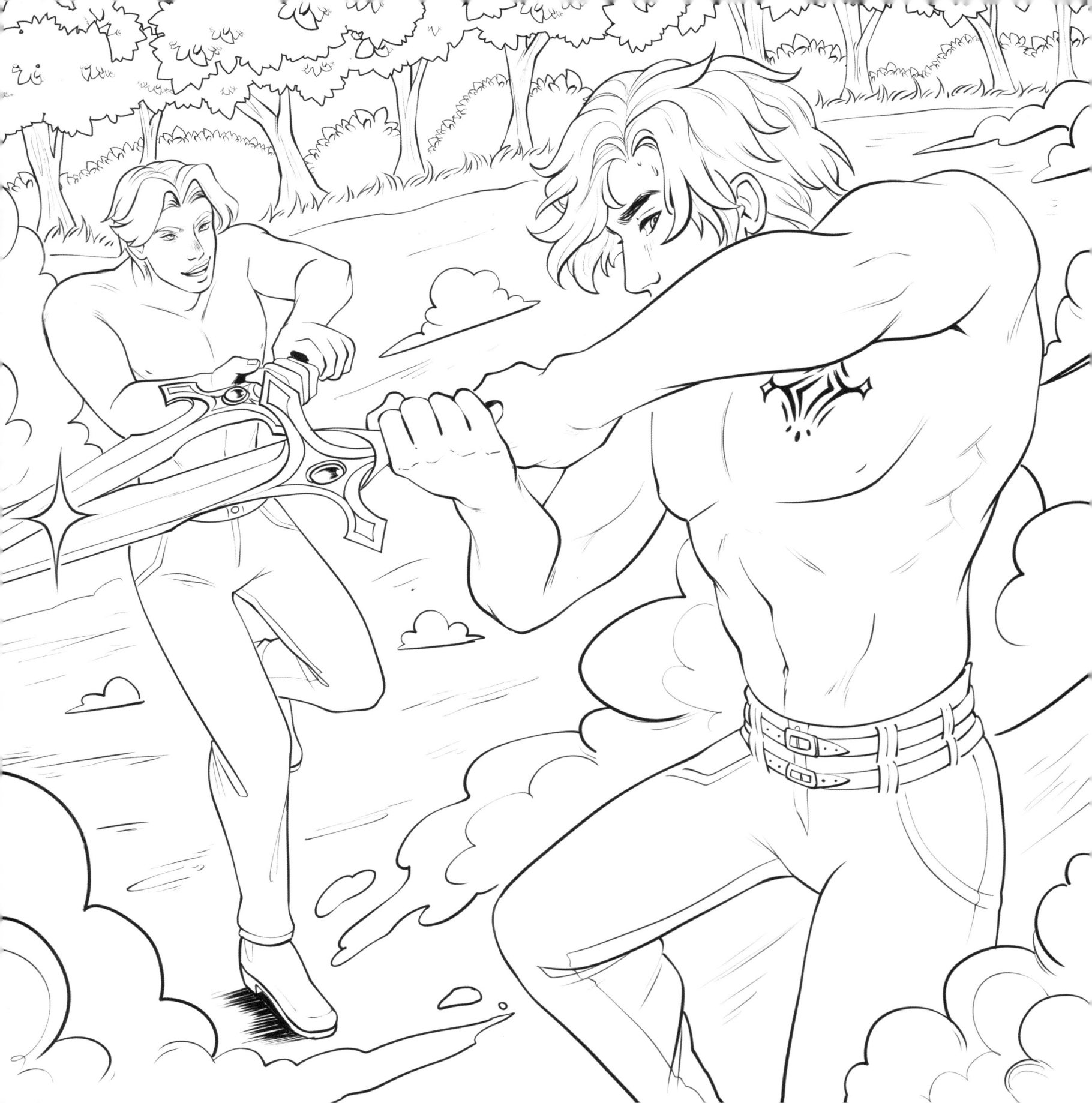

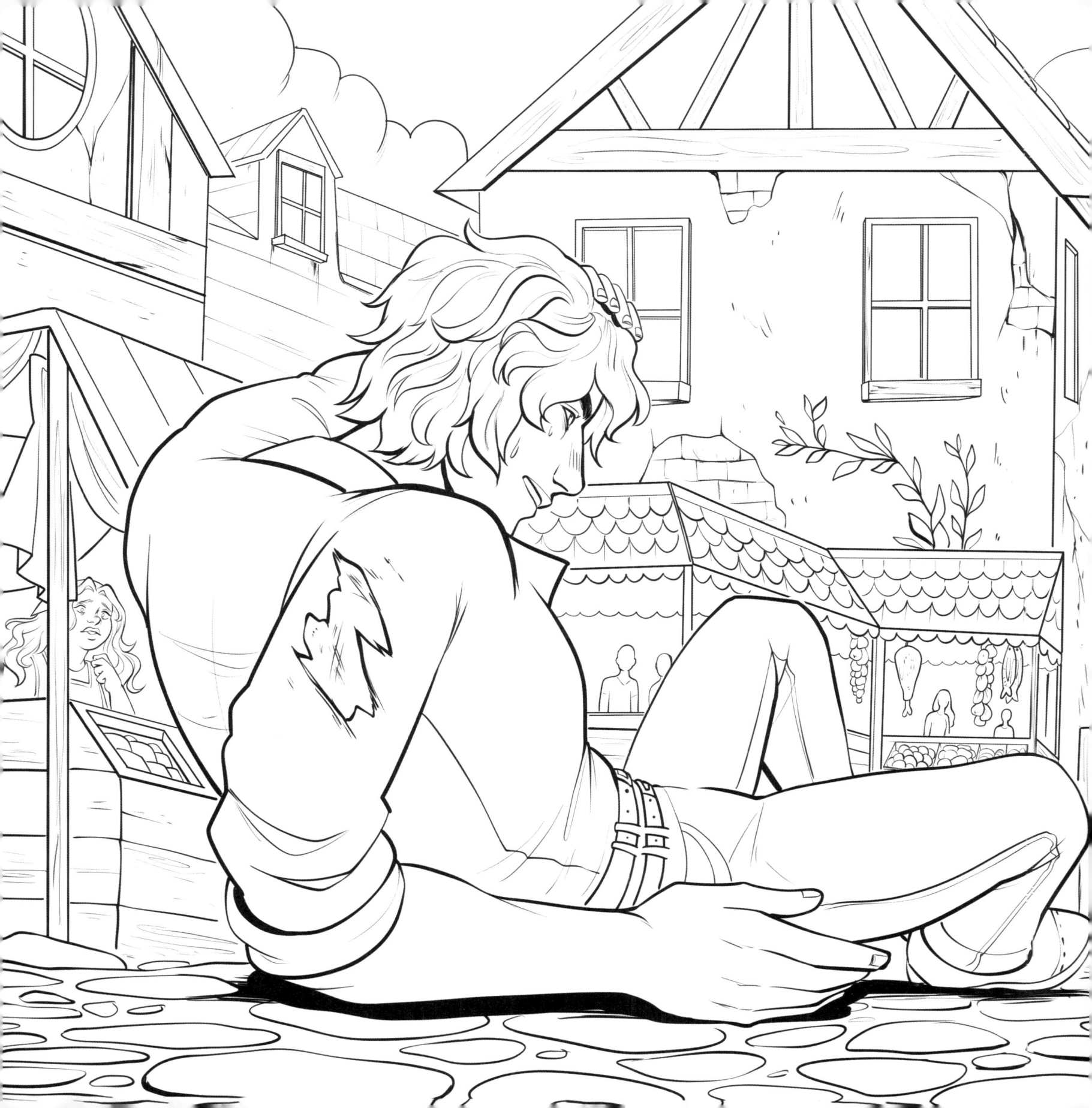

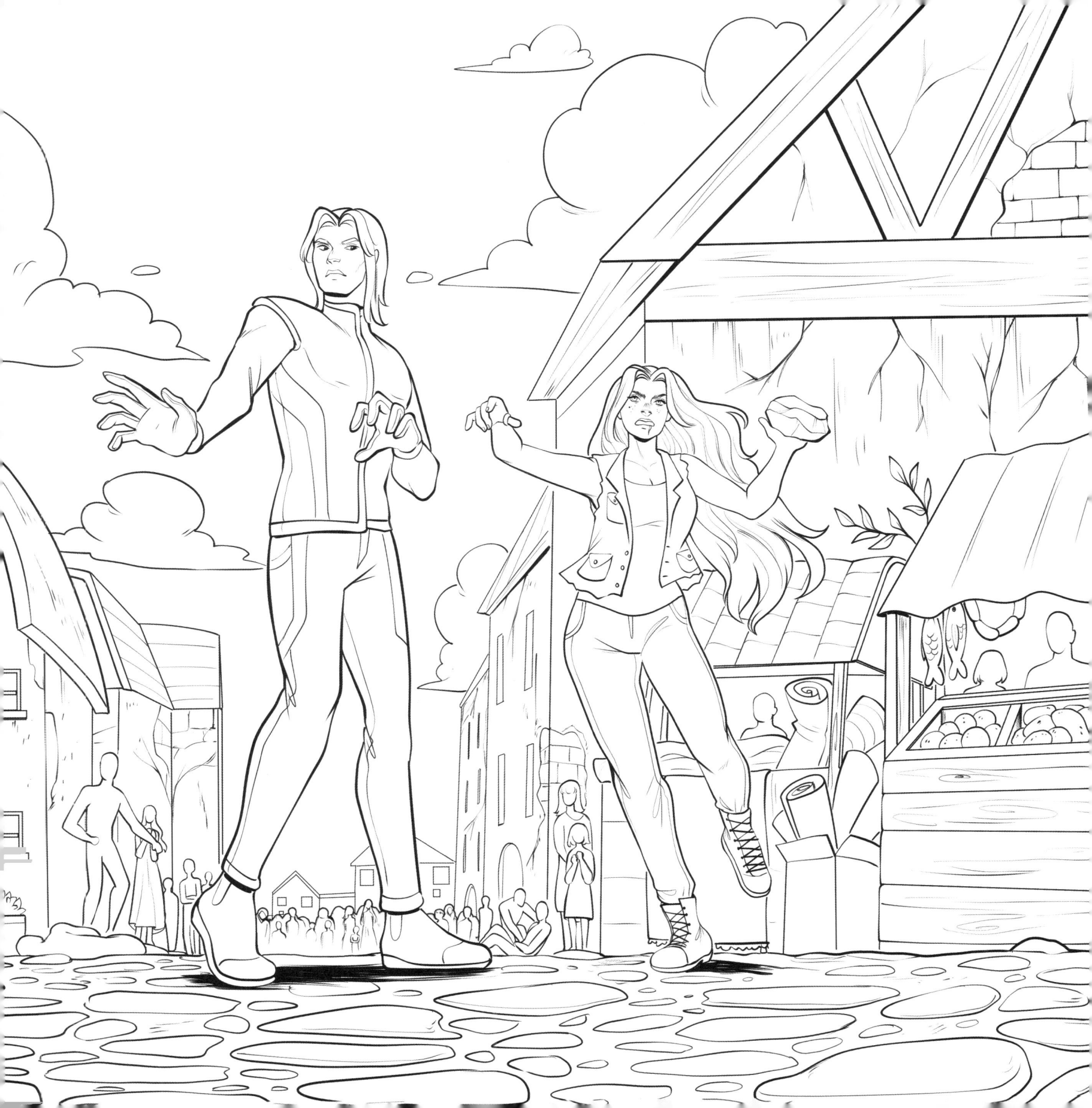

PAEDYN
GRAY

STATUS: ORDINARY

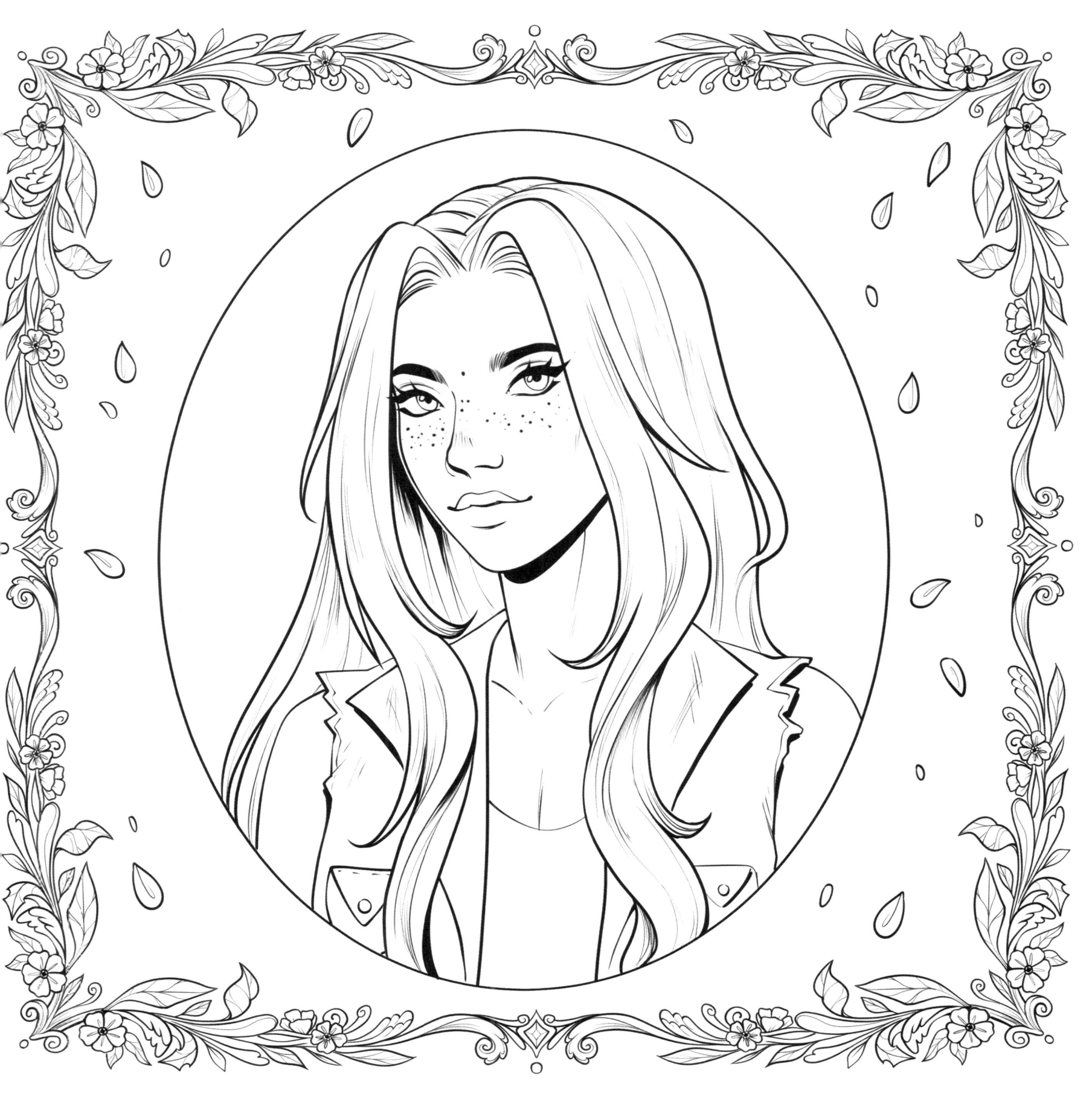

I might have stood there for hours, gawking up at the banner displaying my name in giant letters, if not for the mass of people gawking at me.

They chose me.

Or in other words, they chose me to die.

And all because I saved that prick of a prince.

A tap on my shoulder shakes me from my stupor. I stiffen at the sudden smell of starch and heave a sigh before turning slowly to face the Imperial. He's young. My eyes flick between his messy red hair and brown eyes boring into mine, completely unbothered by my obvious disdain for his kind. He offers me a small, shy smile.

Unsettling.

In all my years, I have never met a kind Imperial, and I doubt he is the exception.

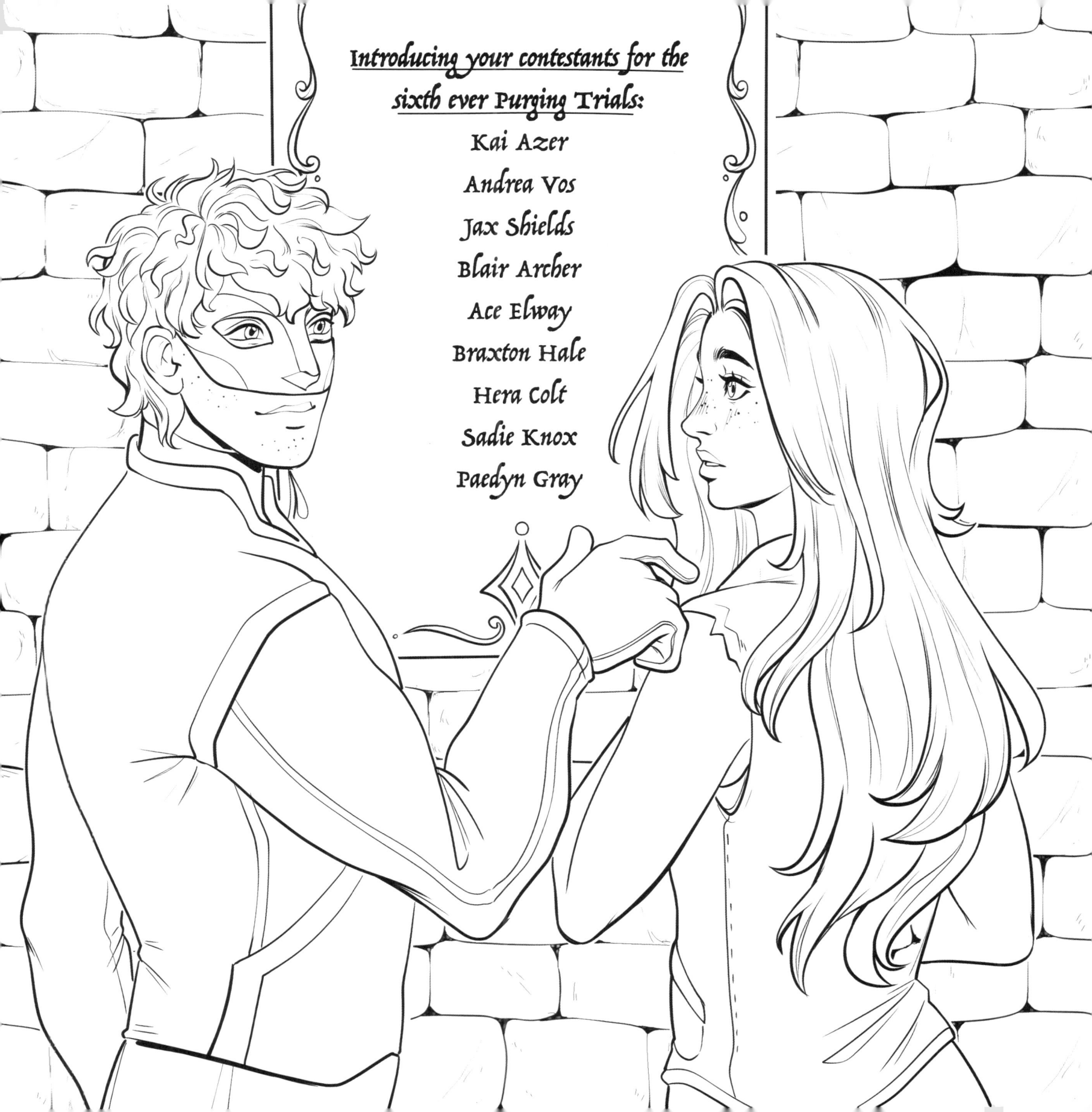

Introducing your contestants for the
sixth ever Purging Trials:

Kai Azer

Andrea Vos

Jax Shields

Blair Archer

Ace Elway

Braxton Hale

Hera Colt

Sadie Knox

Paedyn Gray

KAI
AZER

STATUS: ELITE

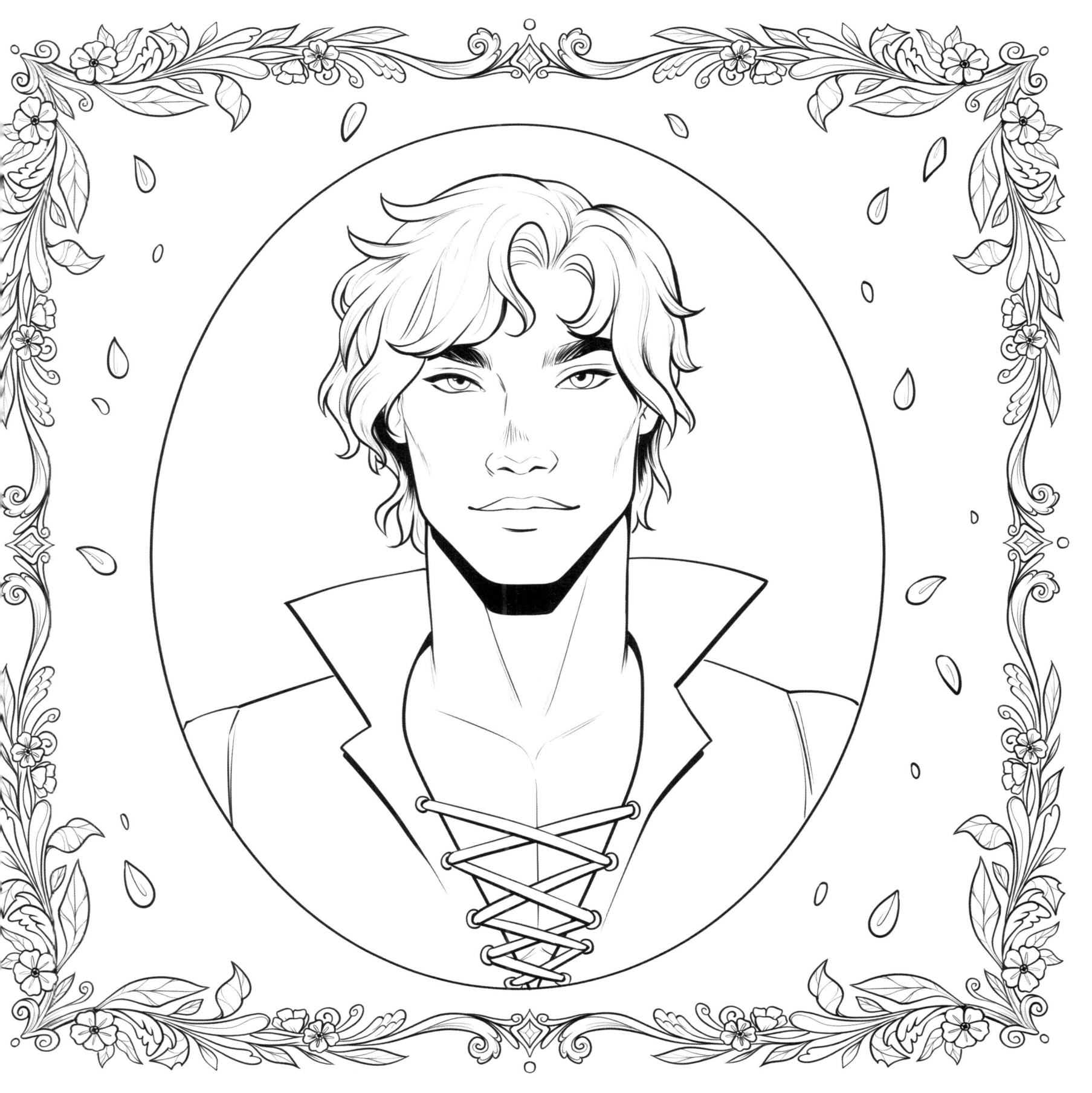

I blink at him.

"Strange," I say slowly. "I don't remember telling you my name."

"Oh, you didn't need to." That crooked grin is teasing his lips once again. "I make it my business to know all the pretty girls who save my little brother."

Plagues, he's—

"I'm Kitt, by the way." He flashes me a grin before turning to stride down the hallway, leaving me shocked and staring.

Prince Kitt. As in "future king of Ilya" Kitt.

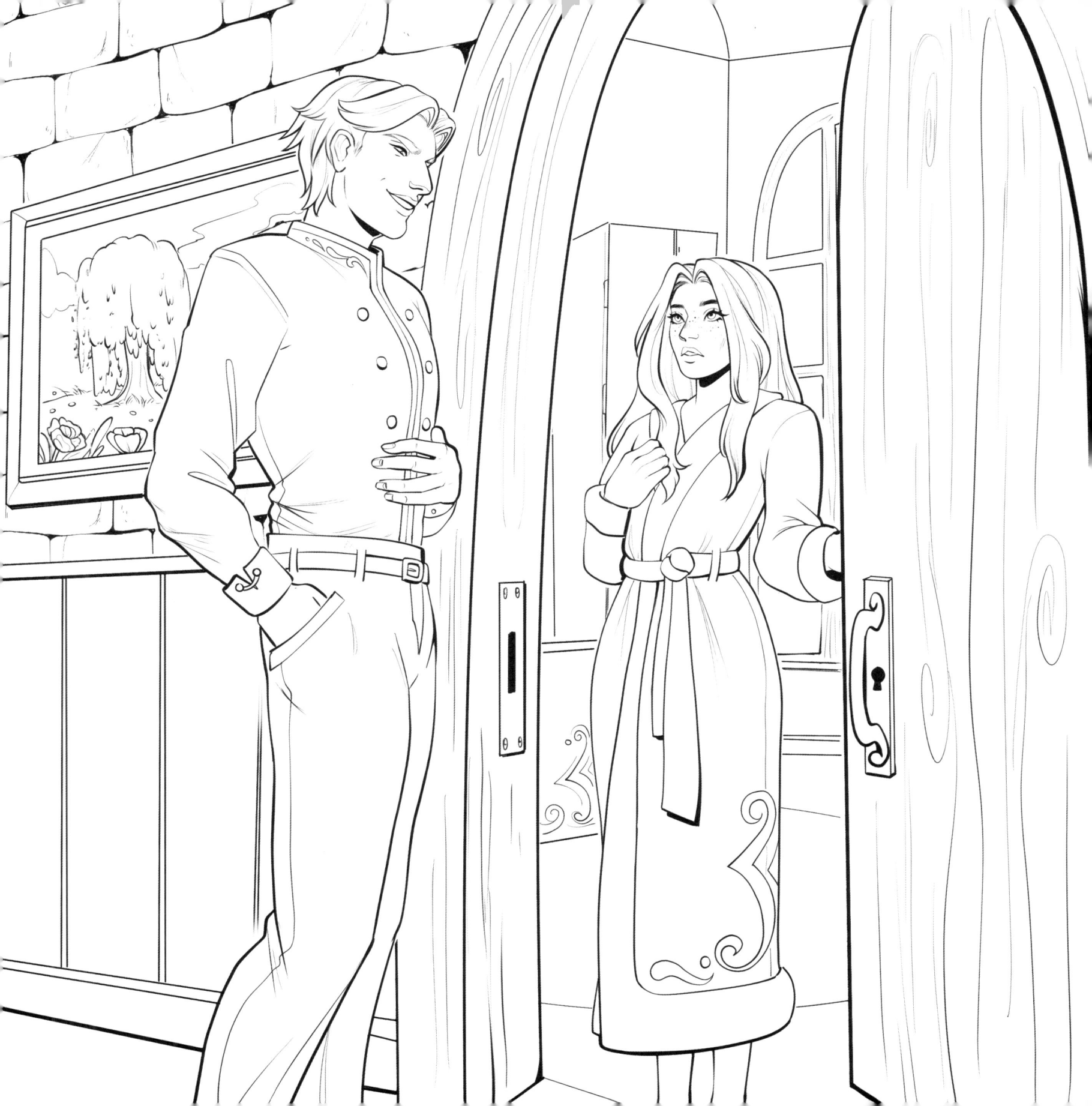

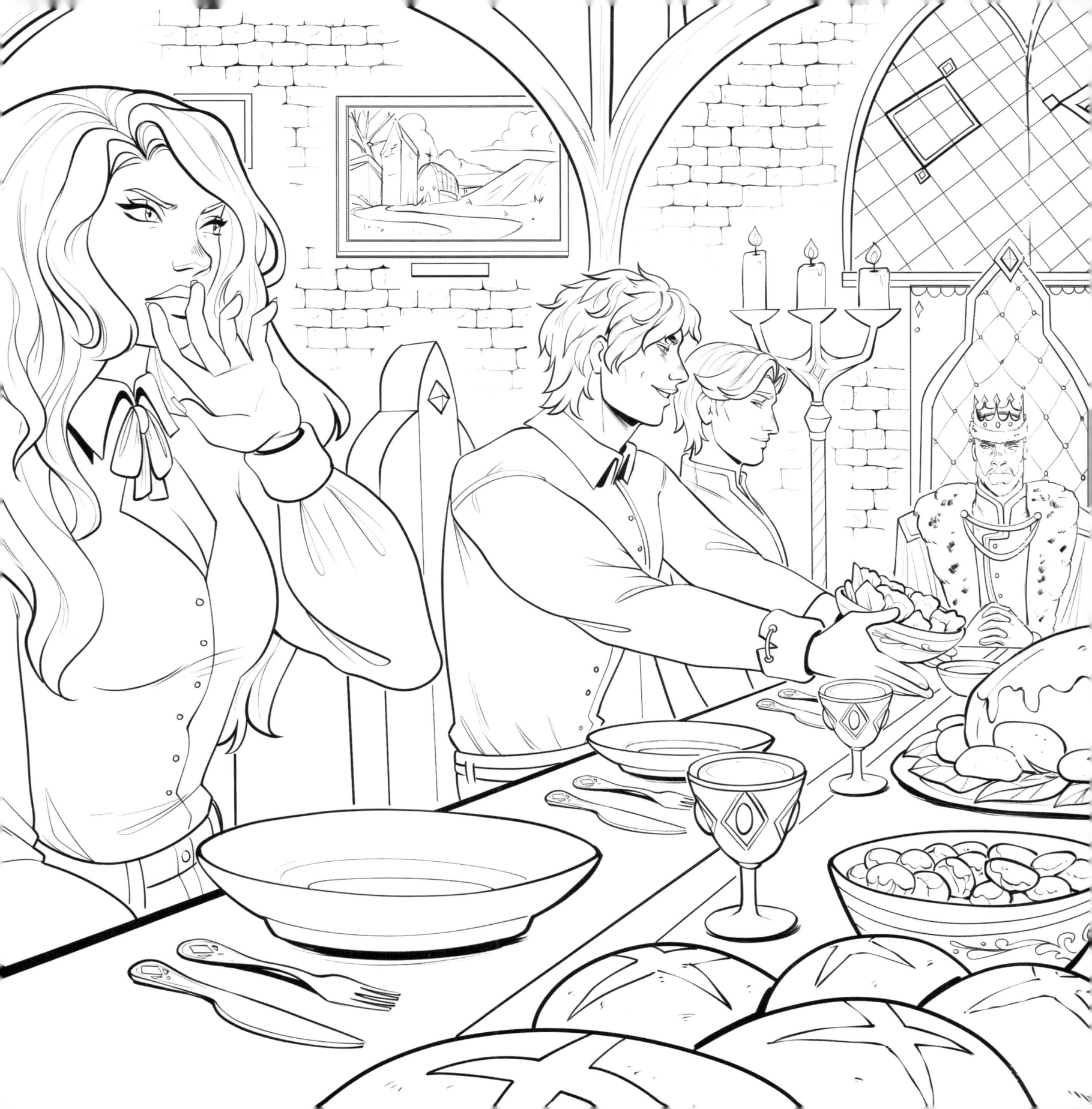

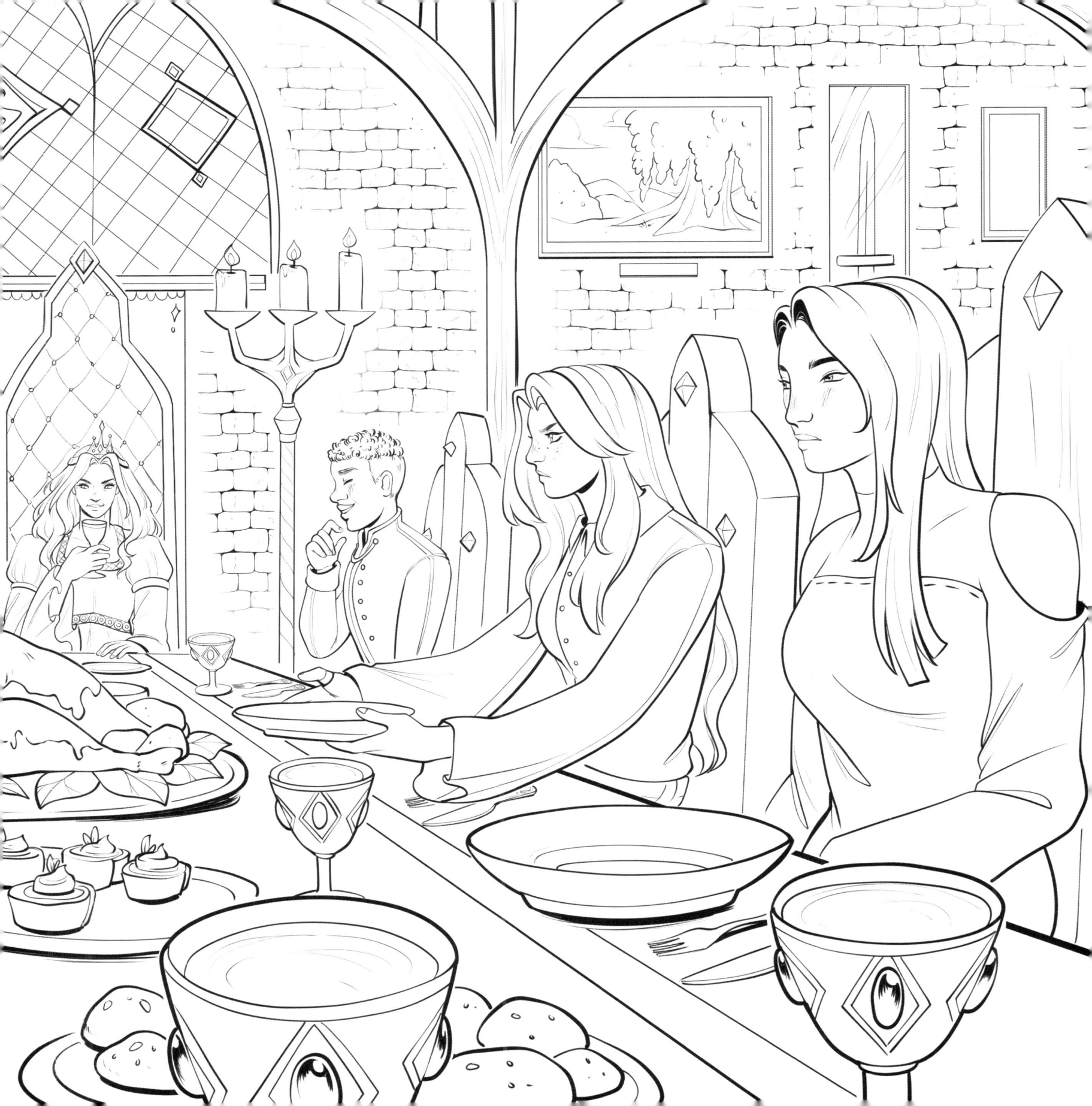

KITT
AZER

STATUS: ELITE

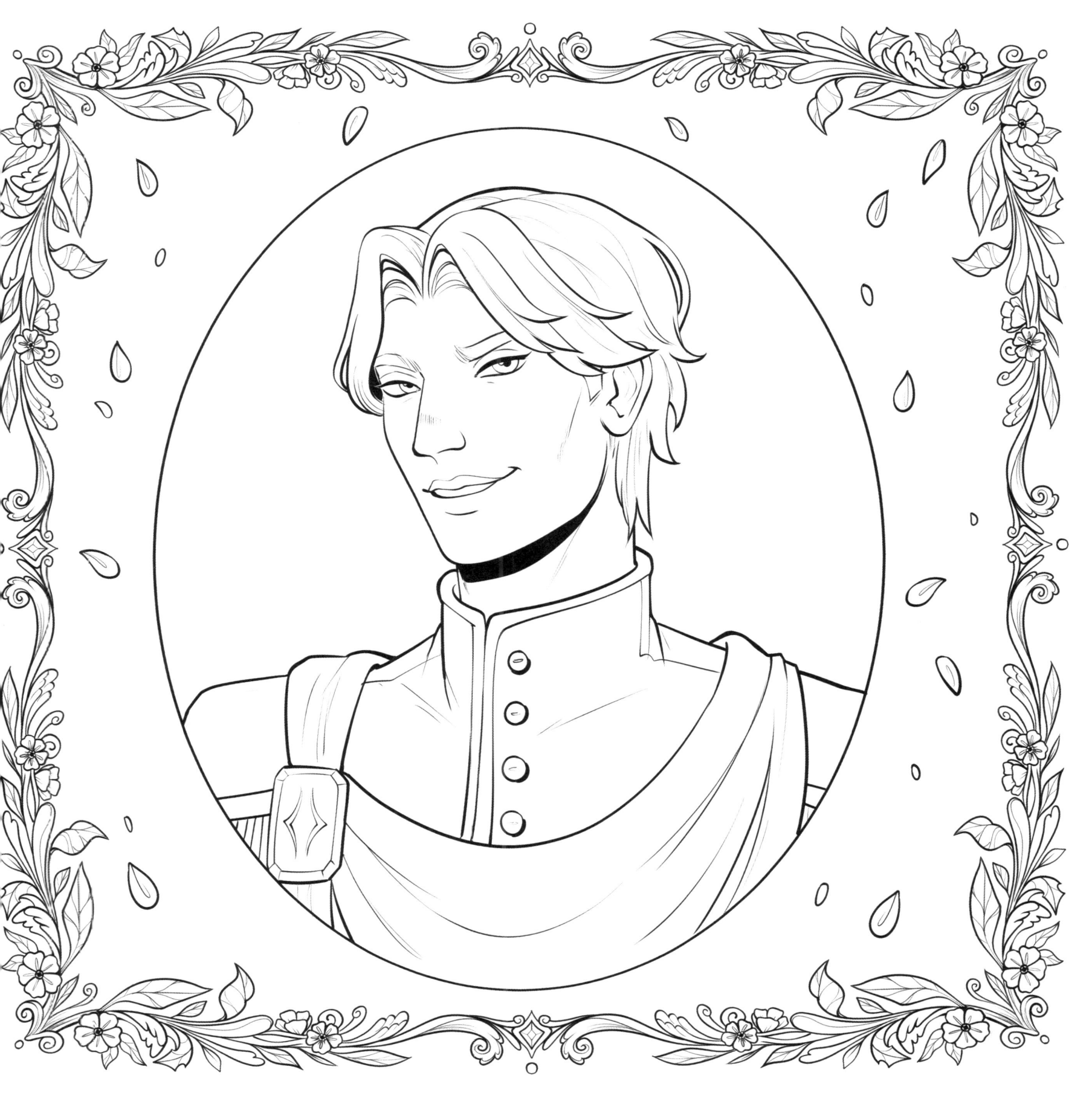

On an impulse I couldn't seem to ignore, my fingers catch her chin and lift her face up toward mine. She's too stunned to move, and I take advantage of it. "I would have thought you could avoid a direct hit like this. Guess you're not as skilled of a fighter as I thought." I shrug and tilt her head toward the light, casually examining the angry cut in her lip.

Oh, but she's no longer standing there stunned, still, and silent.

In one swift movement, she grabs my wrist from under her chin and twists it outward with a jerk, sending a shooting pain up my arm. Then she's gripping my shirt and shoving me against the wall. Her free hand finds the dagger strapped to my hip and slips it out, settling the sharp blade against my throat.

"Would you like to find out just how skilled of a fighter I am?"

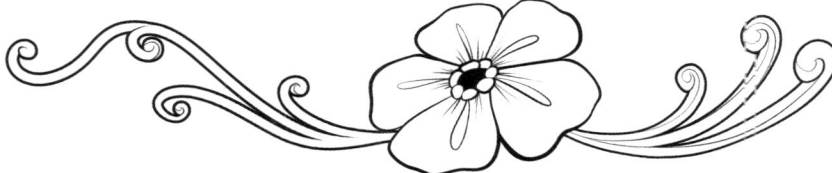

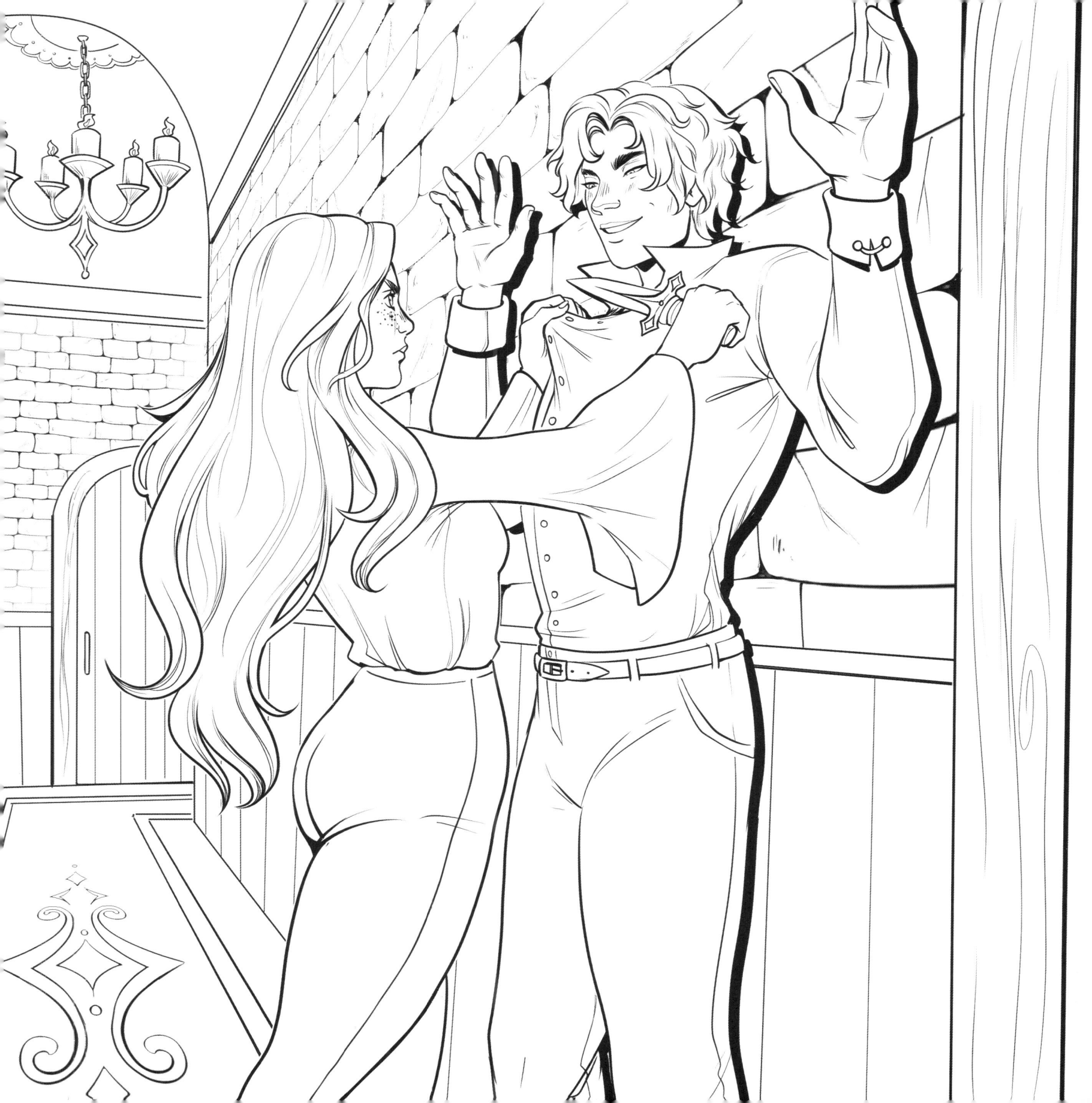

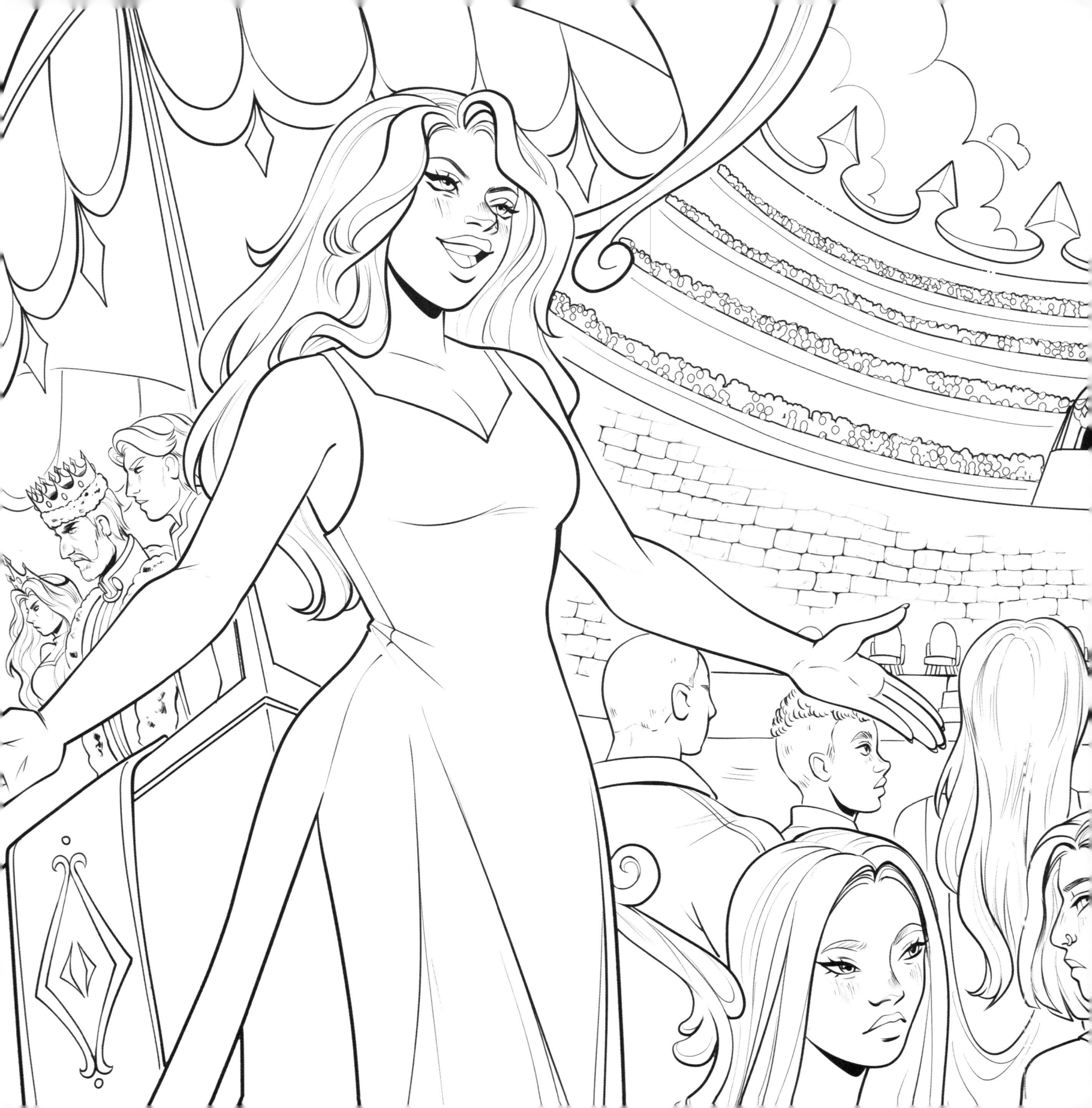

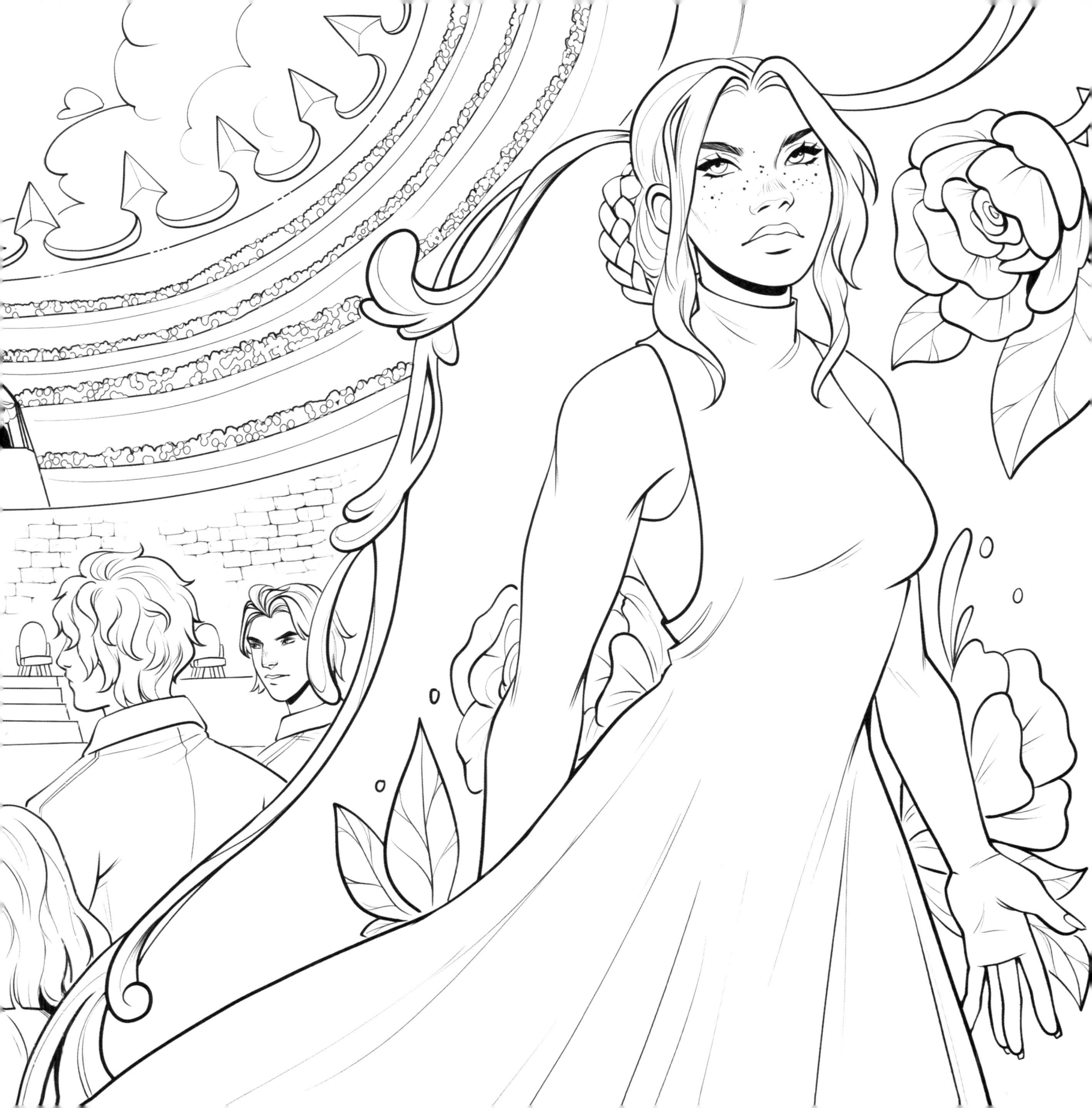

Catching me off guard, she manages to pull my feet from under me, sending the ground flying toward my back.

She's up and on me in a second, practically jumping on top of my chest, placing her knees on either side of me. And then she cocks a bloody fist back, her smile triumphant.

I take her in, bloody and straddling me. "If it weren't for my current situation," I glance at her fist still posed to strike, "this could be a lot more fun," I say quietly, looking her up and down before staring into those blue eyes as they widen.

Her focus slips for a moment.

Perfect.

I grab her waist and flip us over. Now I'm on top of her, pinning her wrists into the dirt beside her head. She pants beneath me, glaring up into my face.

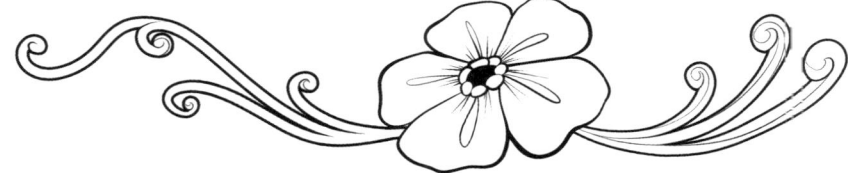

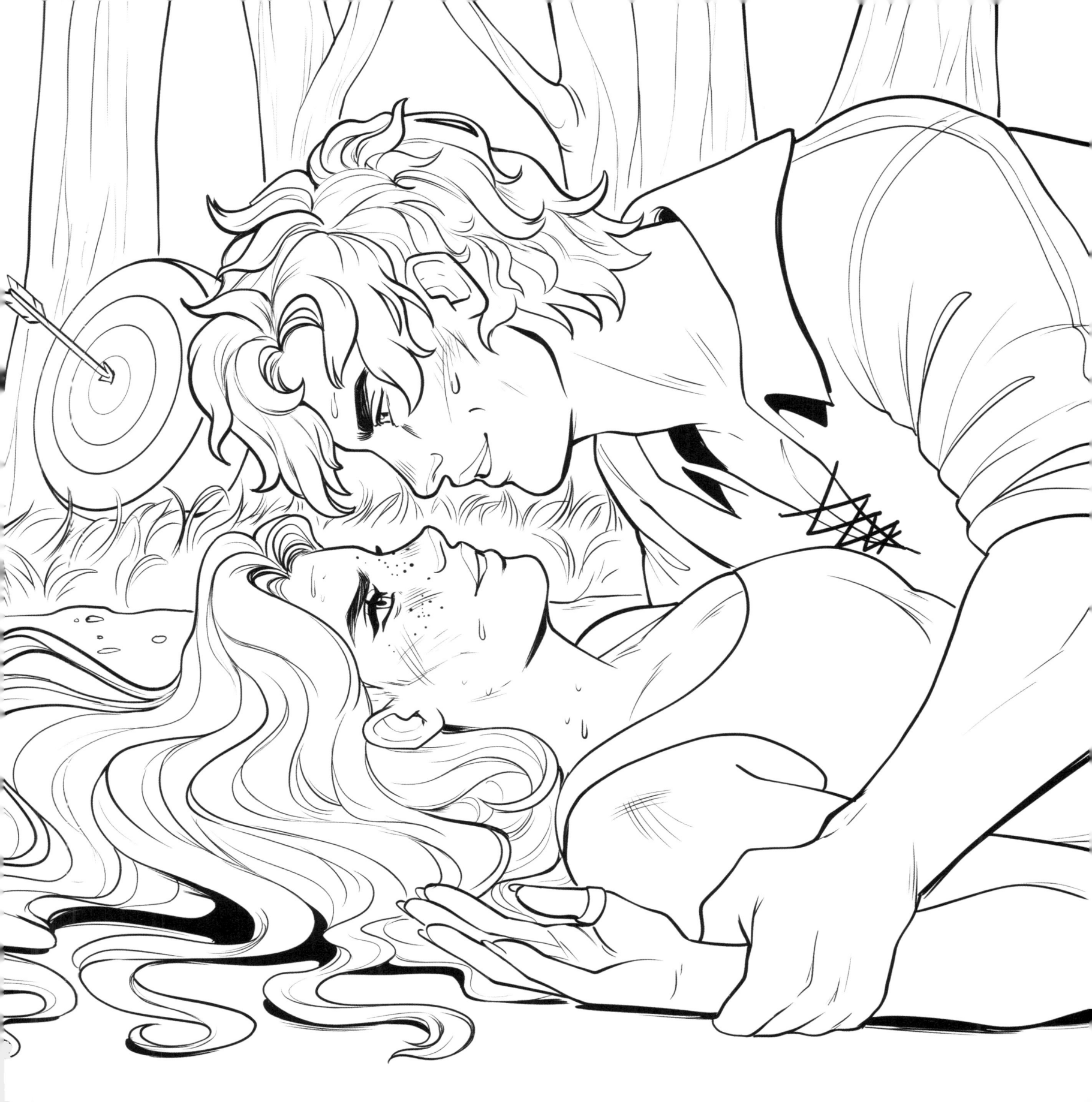

ADENA

STATUS: ELITE

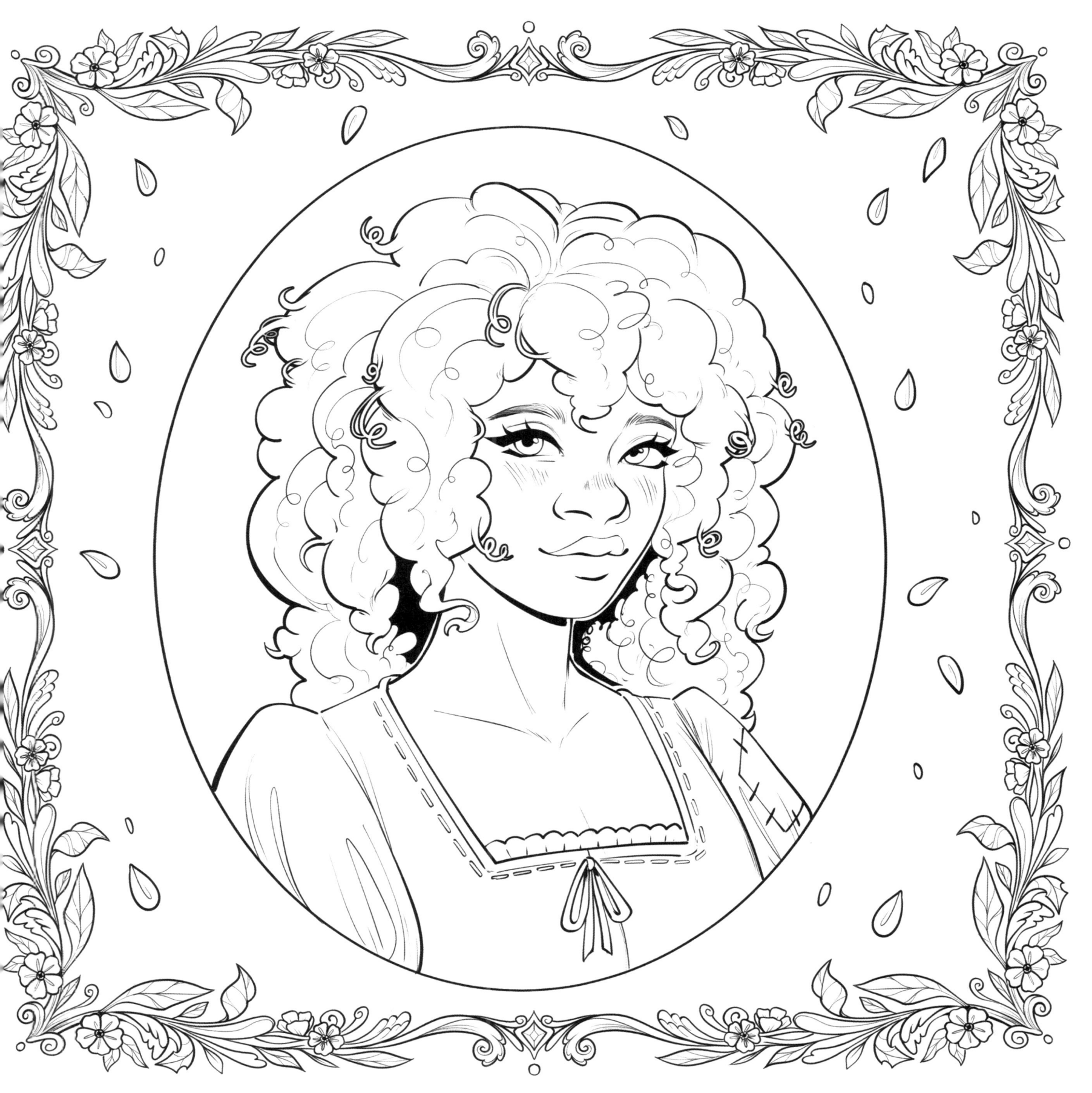

"Knives are also not necessary for dancing," Kai says with a low laugh.

Holding my gaze, his rough fingers slide slowly from my wrist to my palm before he folds his hand into mine, raising it into the air.

But it's his other hand that holds my attention, the one that has settled comfortably against the small of my back. The one that is pulling me toward him. Through the thin fabric of the dress I threw on for dinner, I can feel the warmth of his palm seeping into my lower back.

I stare at him as he pulls me close. It's not as if I didn't know this was bound to happen—I just wasn't expecting it so suddenly.

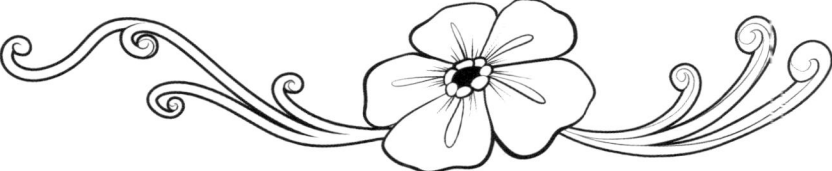

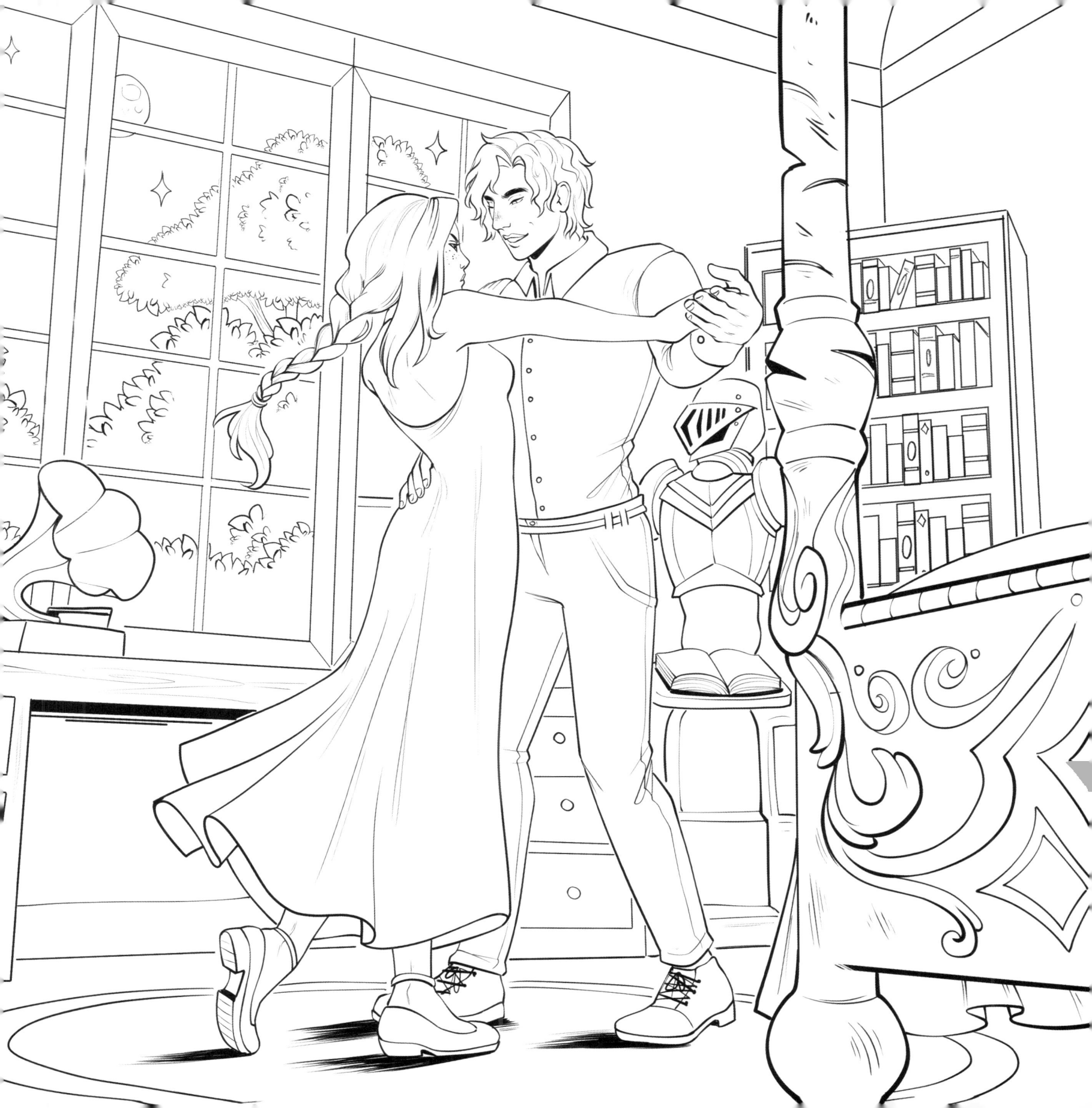

"It sounds like Ellie and I will get along perfectly," Adena says, her smile bright.

"Oh, I'm sure you will." I laugh before continuing, "And you will be paid, fed, and have a real bed to sleep in at night. I'm told there is a sewing room where you will spend most of your time, filled with every type of fabric you could ever dream of."

Adena's eyes go glossy at the thought. "Heaven. I'll be in heaven." I fill her in on everything—the training, the interviews, the contestants. She does the same, telling me of her time on Loot while I've been gone.

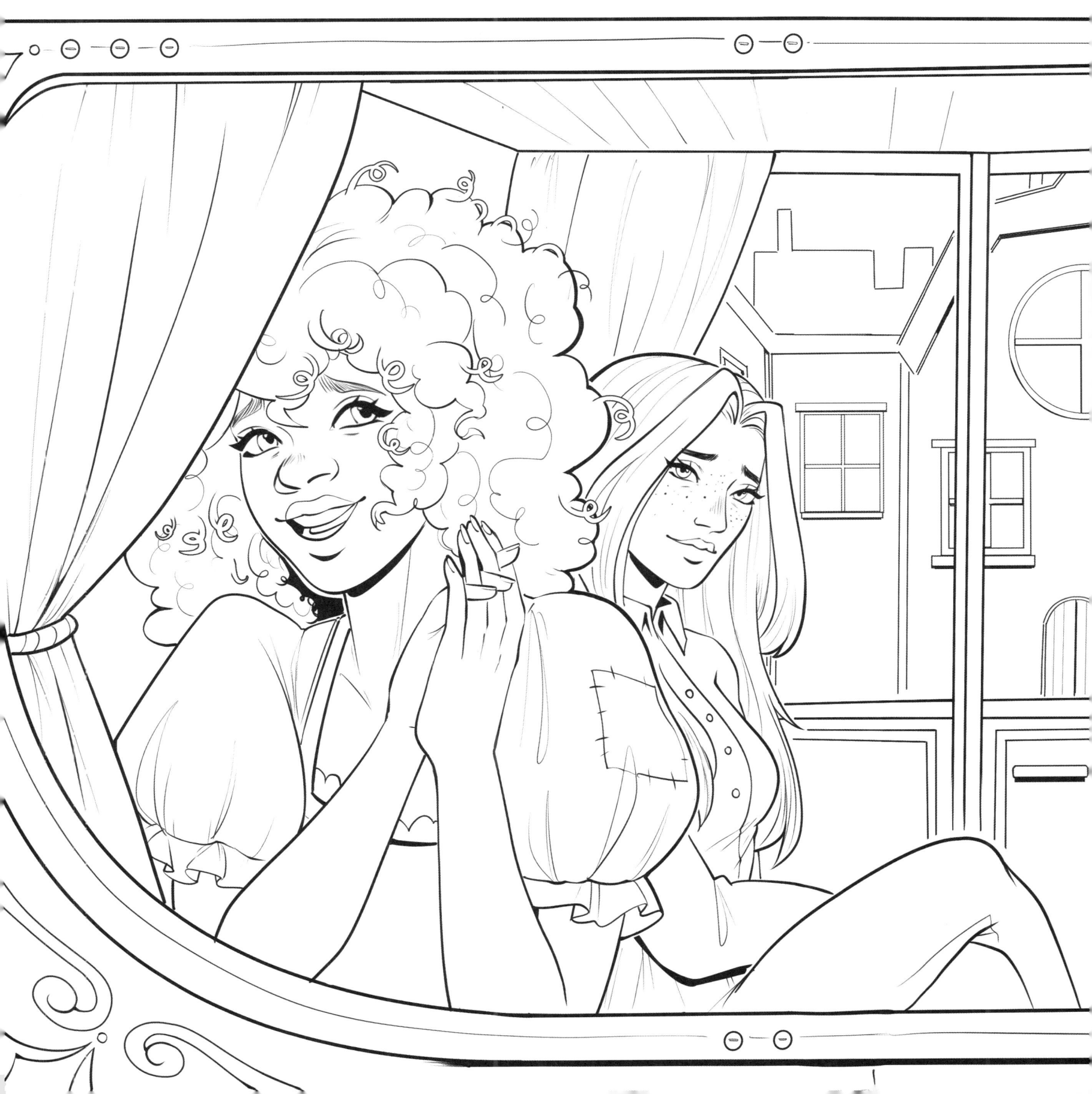

Explosives erupt around the room, and my ears ring from the impact. I feel a wave of heat accompanied by smoke and hunks of stone sailing toward us.

Kai's large frame hovers over me, his hand cradling the back of my head so my skull didn't crack on the hard marble when he threw us to the ground. He's shielding my body from the debris and knives flying around the room. I regain my hearing slowly, each scream amplifying as my ears pop and ring back to life. I hear terror and the trampling of feet all around us, men and women rushing toward the exits, trying to escape the madness.

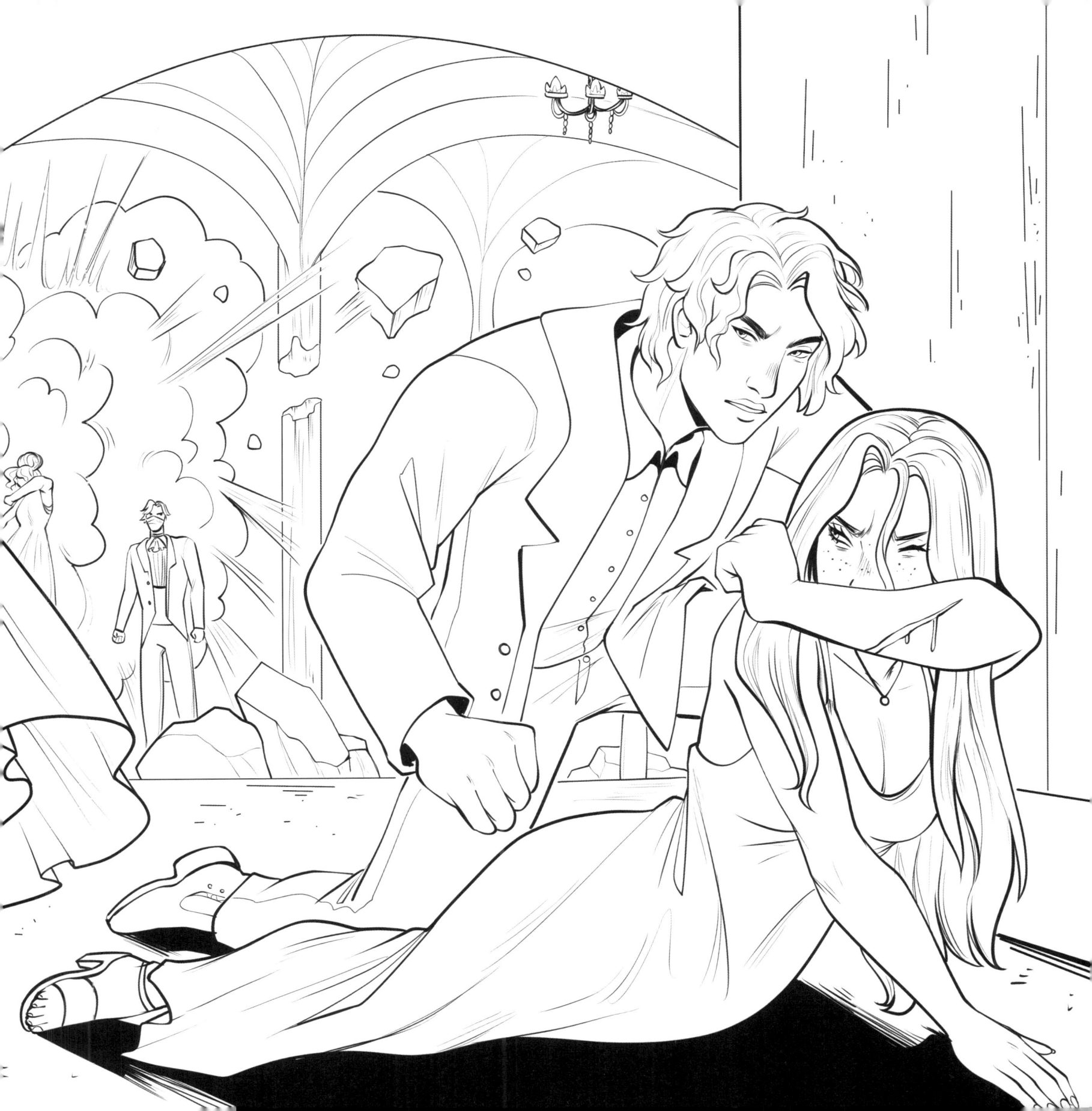

EDRIC AZER

STATUS: ELITE

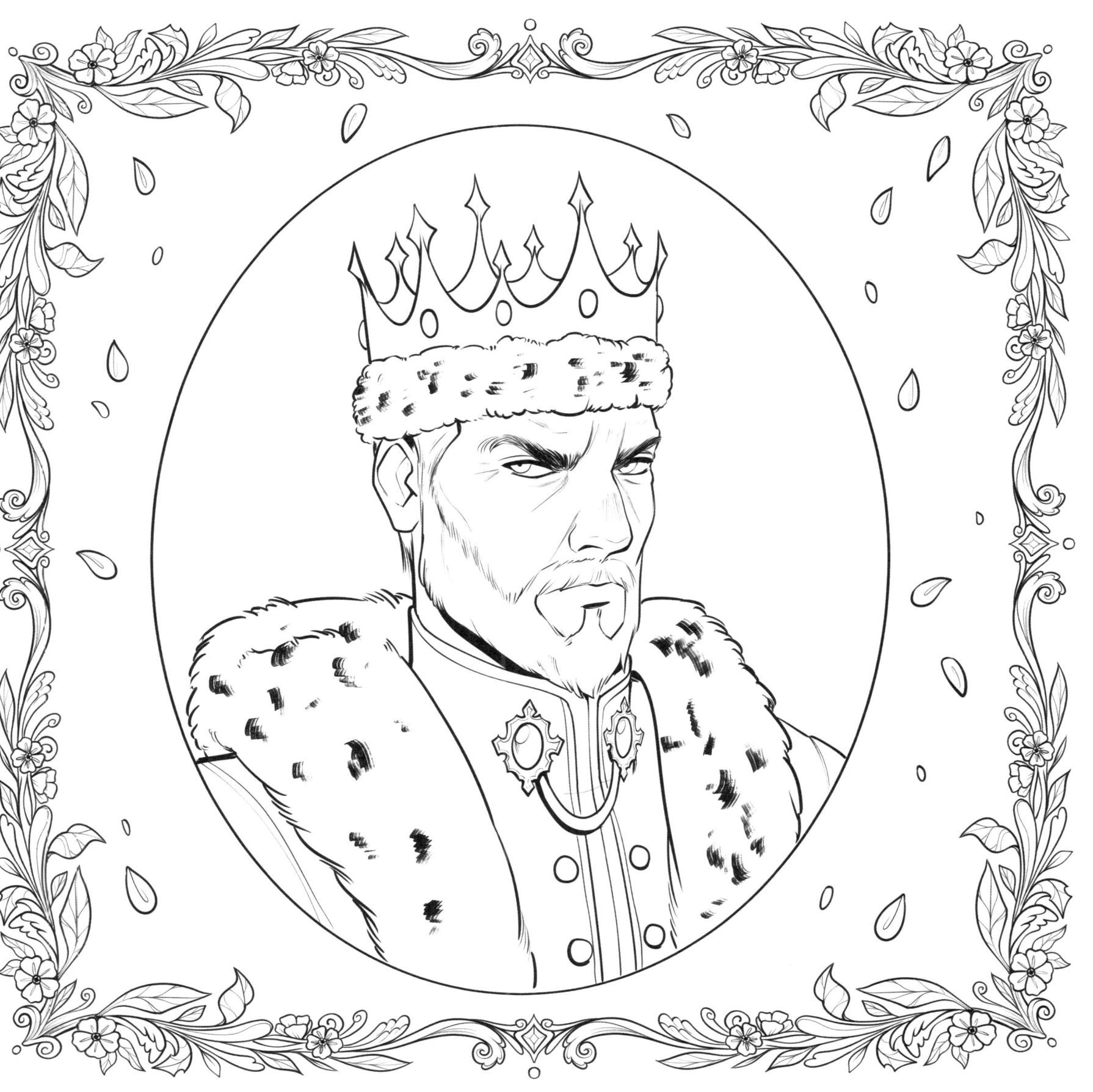

Kitt clears his throat and leans away from me. "They call themselves the Resistance." His voice is low and steady, intended for only me to hear. "They are a group of Ordinaries that have been banding together for years. Fighting against the king and the kingdom because of what was done to their kind."

Their kind. My kind.

I force myself to swallow my disgust and listen as he continues. "At first, they were barely a threat, a joke of a revolution. We've kept this little group a secret, kept it hidden from the people for a few years now. It hasn't been hard to do till recently. But clearly, they are bigger and stronger than before."

I think I stopped breathing. All I hear is the blood pounding in my ears as I take in the weight of his words.

A group of Ordinaries fighting against the king and the kingdom.

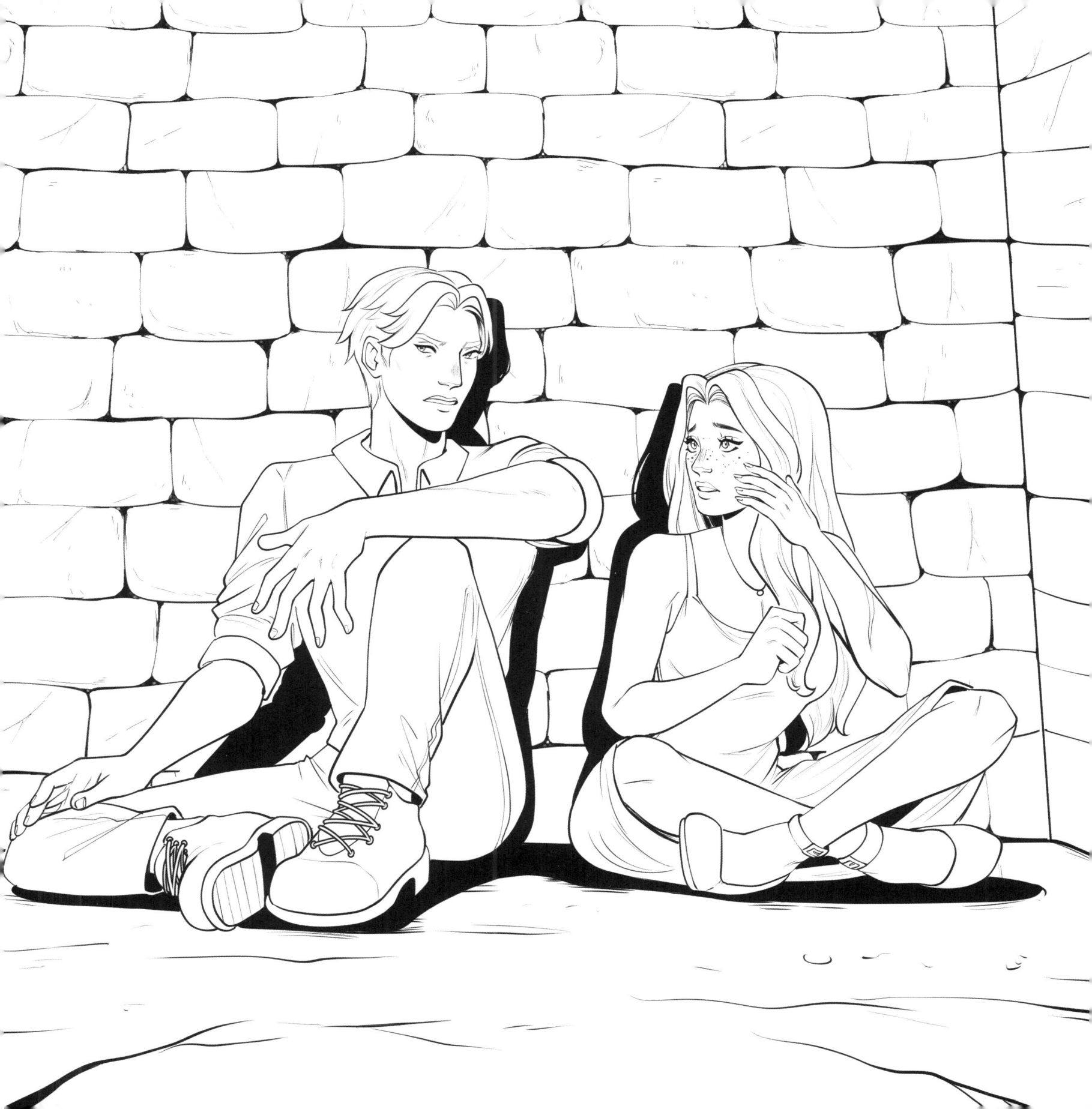

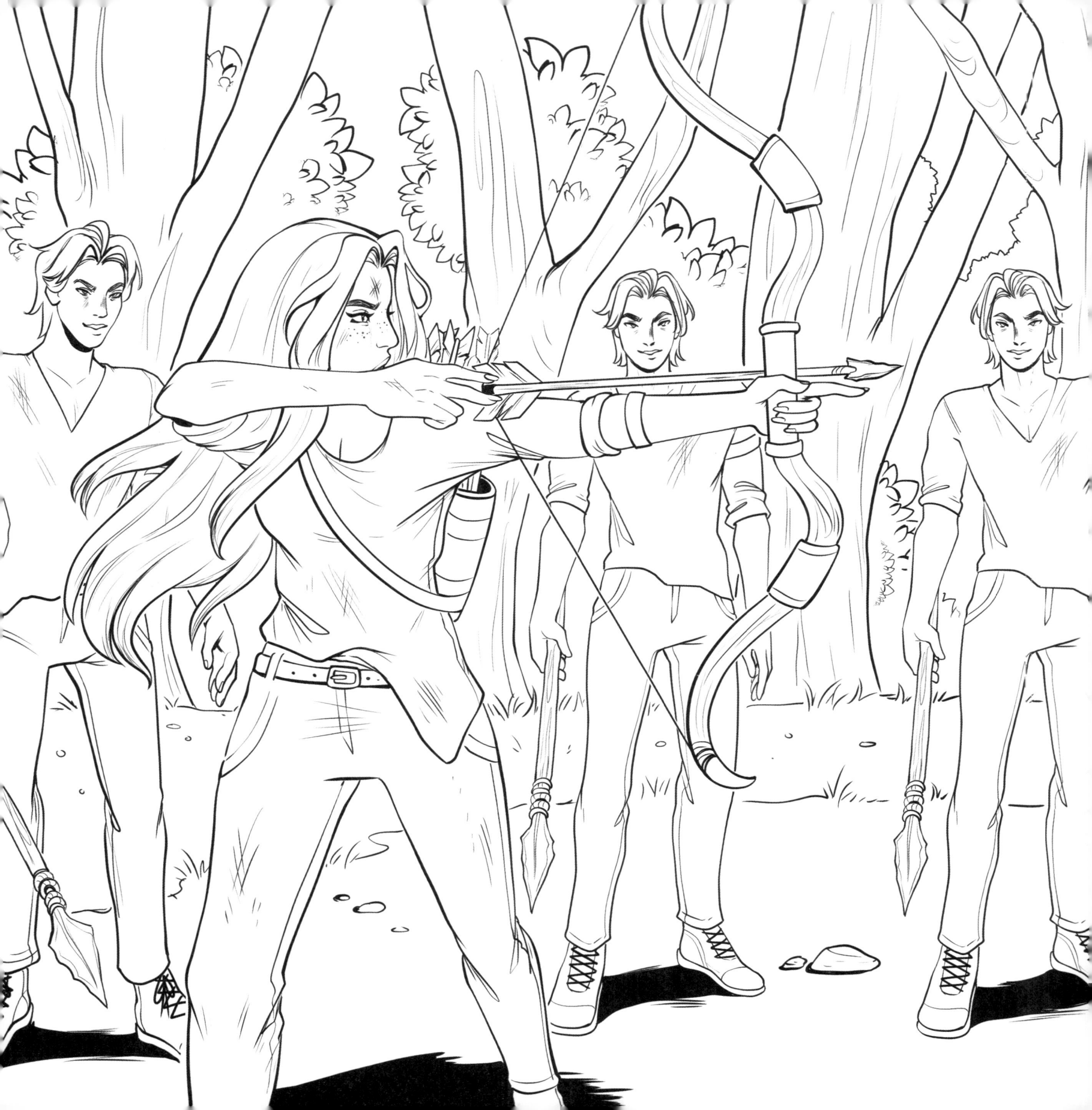

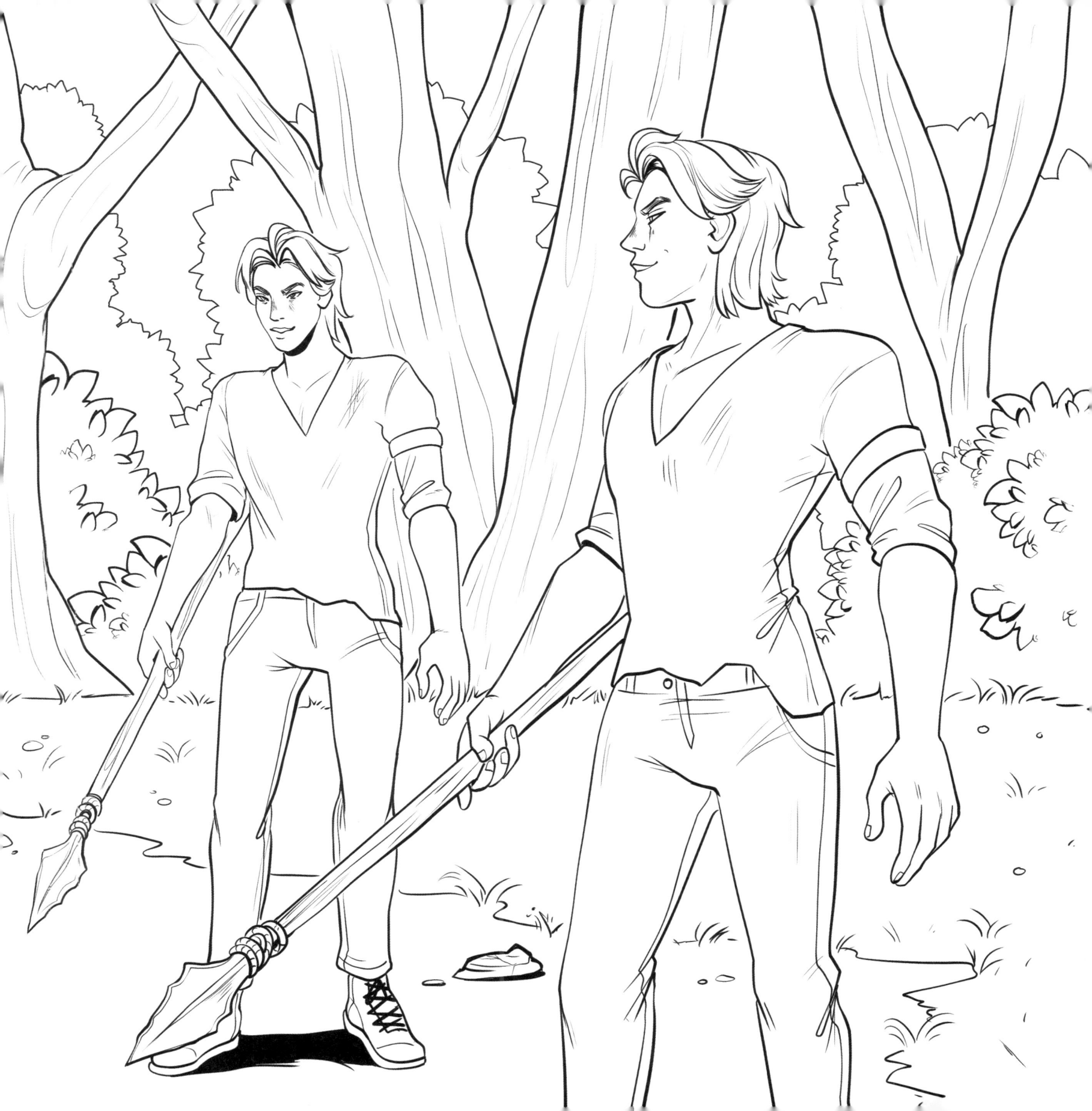

JAX
SHIELDS

STATUS: ELITE

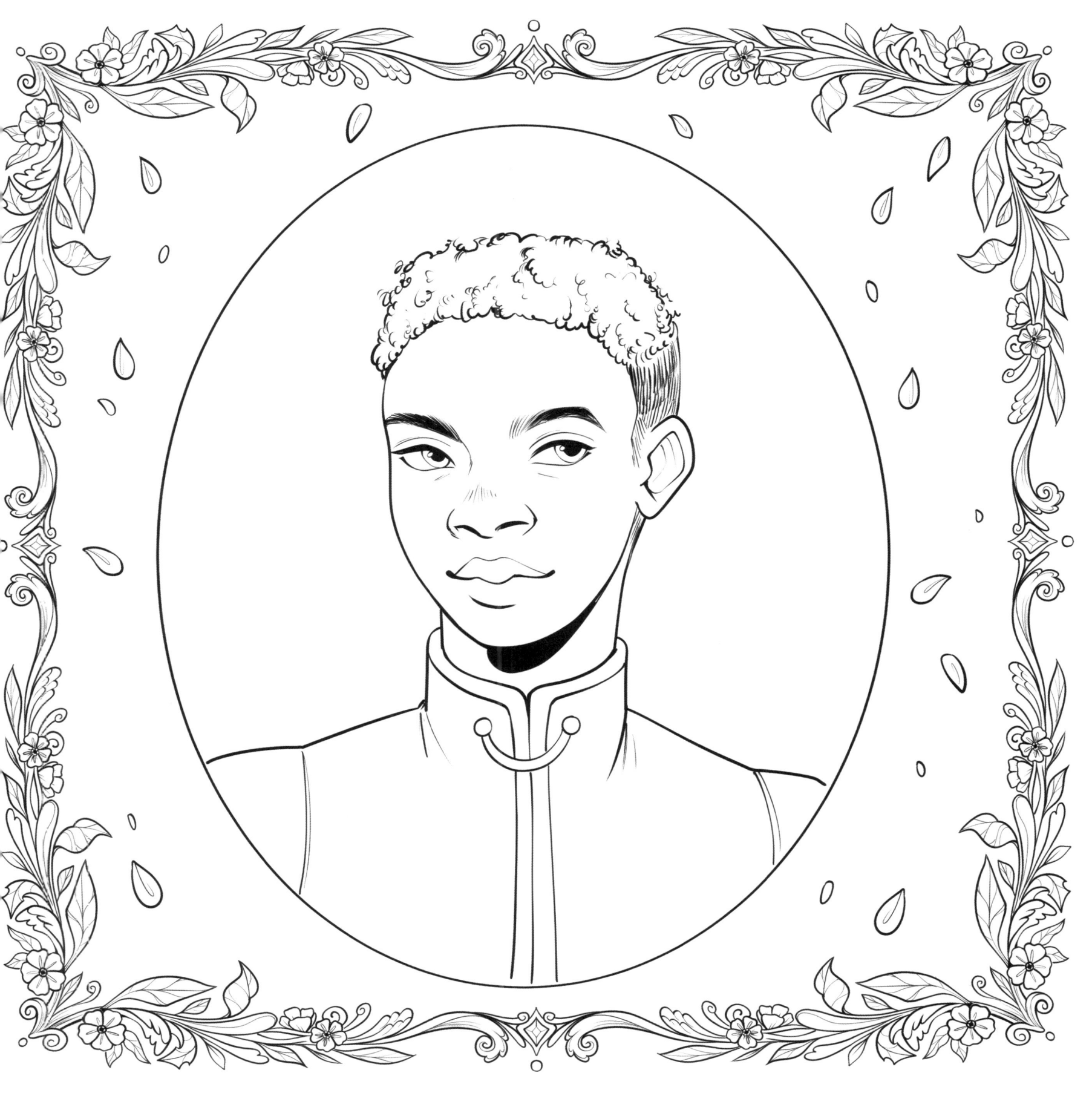

I spin her if only to give myself some time to think. I'd never thought about what my favorite color was before. It never seemed important.

Not until I looked into a pair of ocean-blue eyes and realized that perhaps drowning was a beautiful thing.

Not until I looked into a pair of fiery blue eyes and realized that perhaps burning was a painless thing.

Not until I looked into a pair of sky-blue eyes and realized that perhaps falling was a peaceful thing.

I'd never thought about what my favorite color was before because I hadn't seen one that was worthy of the title. Until now, that is.

"Blue," I say, my voice low.

"Hmm." She's looking at me thoughtfully, studying me sincerely. "I would have never guessed."

Neither would I.

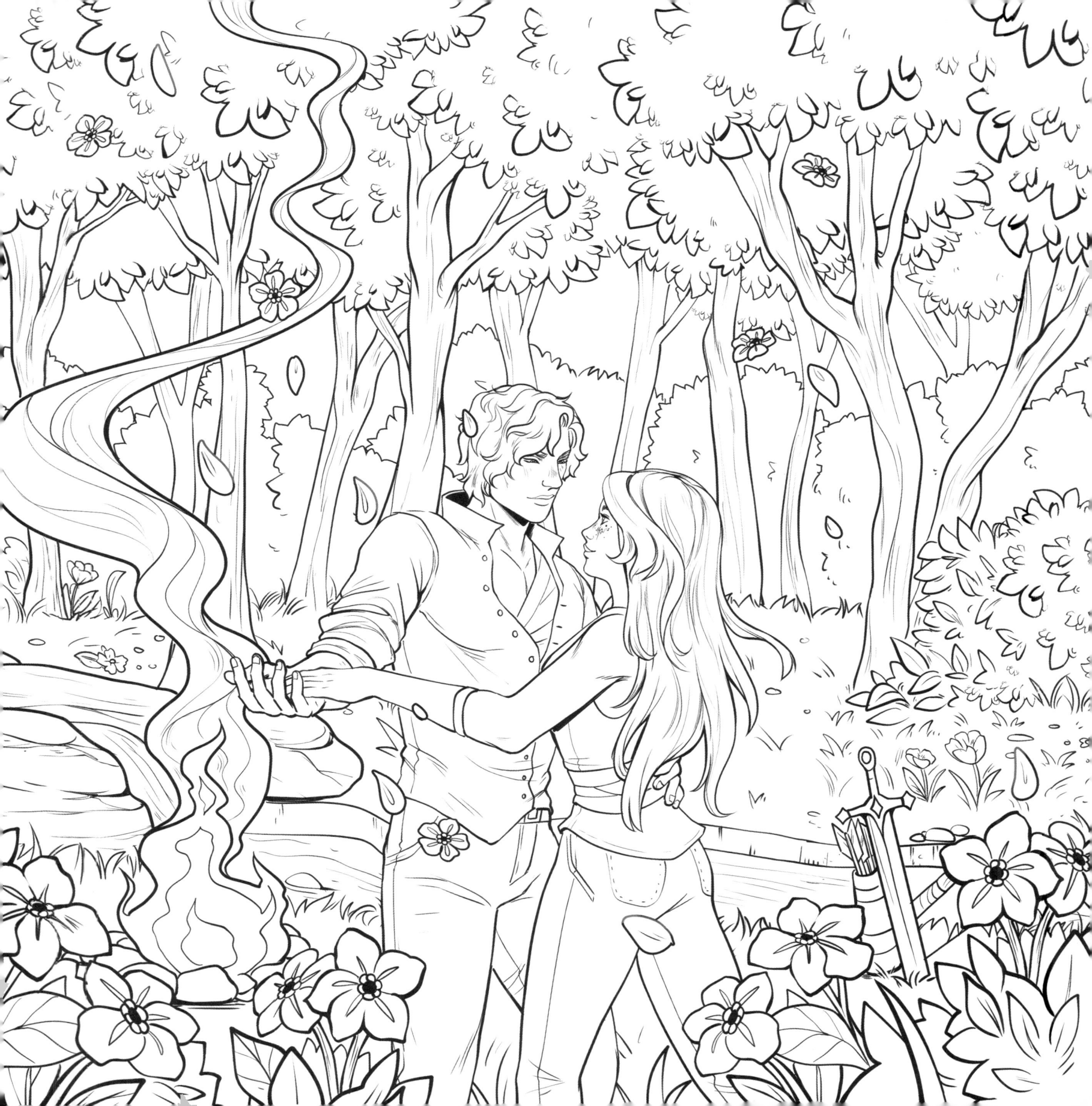

BLAIR
ARCHER

STATUS: ELITE

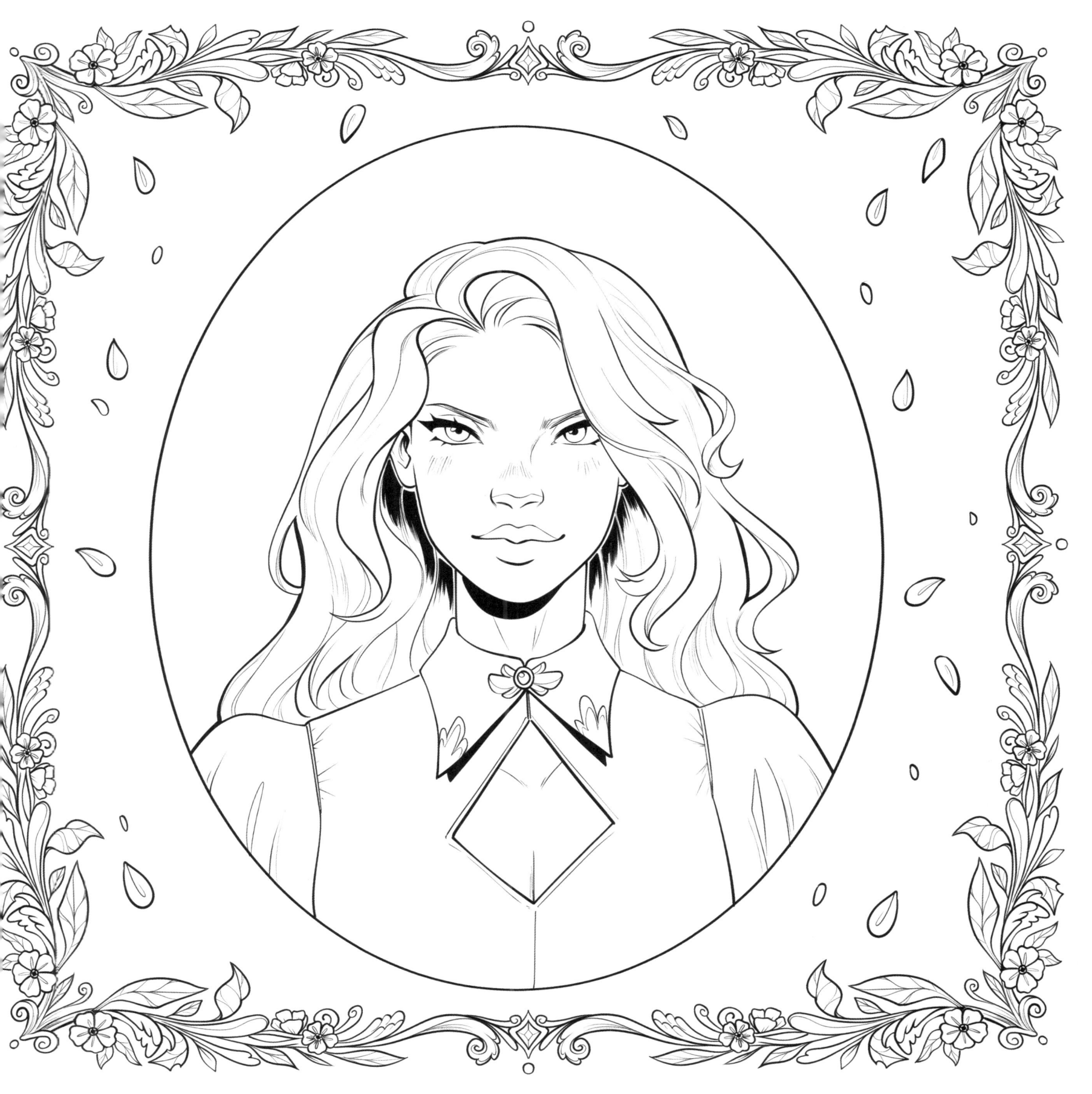

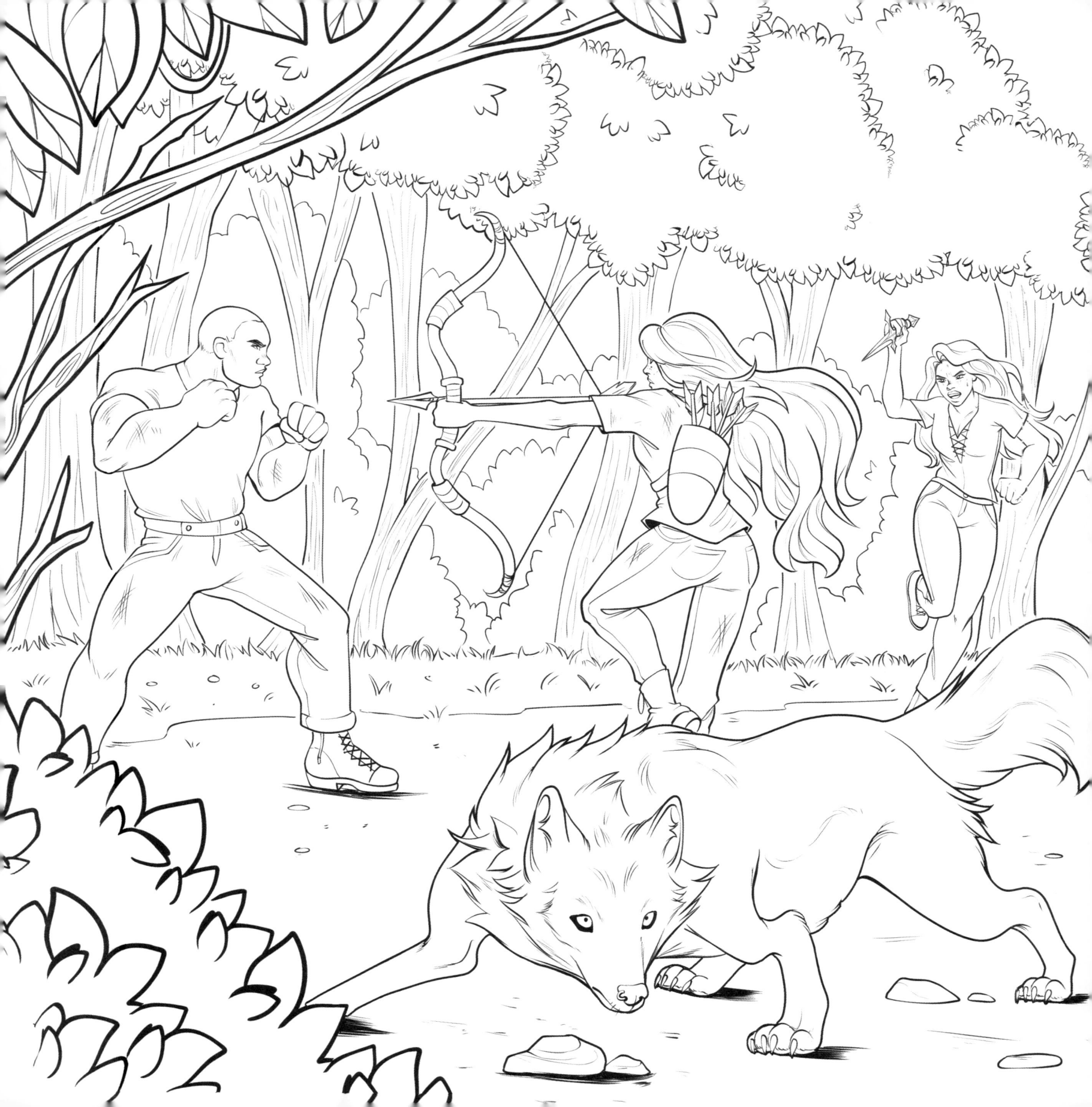

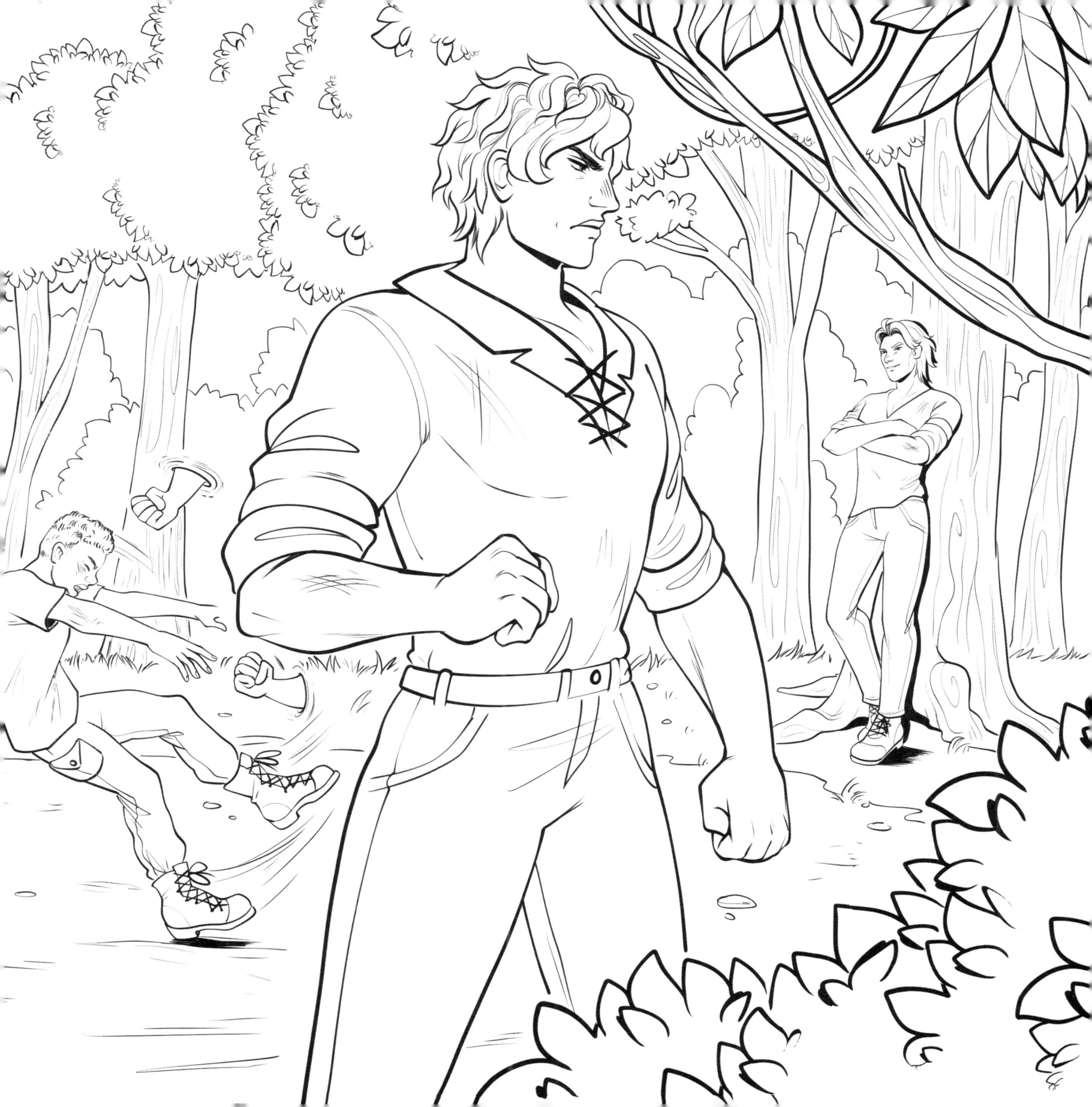

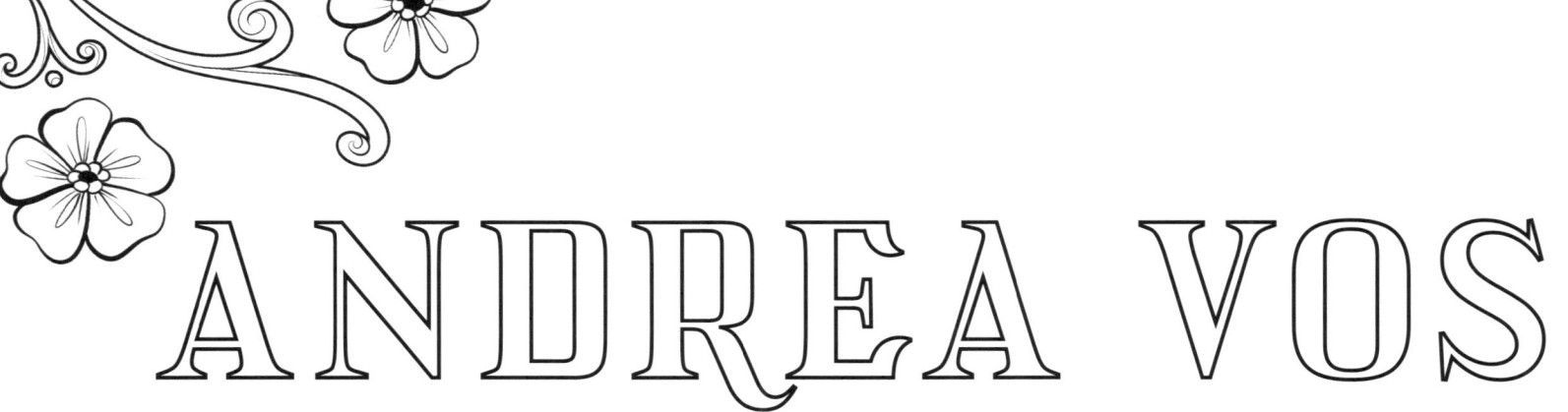

ANDREA VOS

STATUS: ELITE

SADIE KNOX

STATUS: ELITE

HERA COLT

STATUS: ELITE

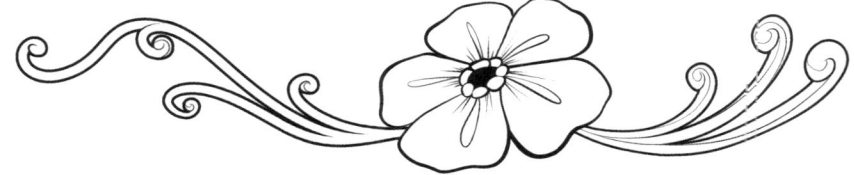

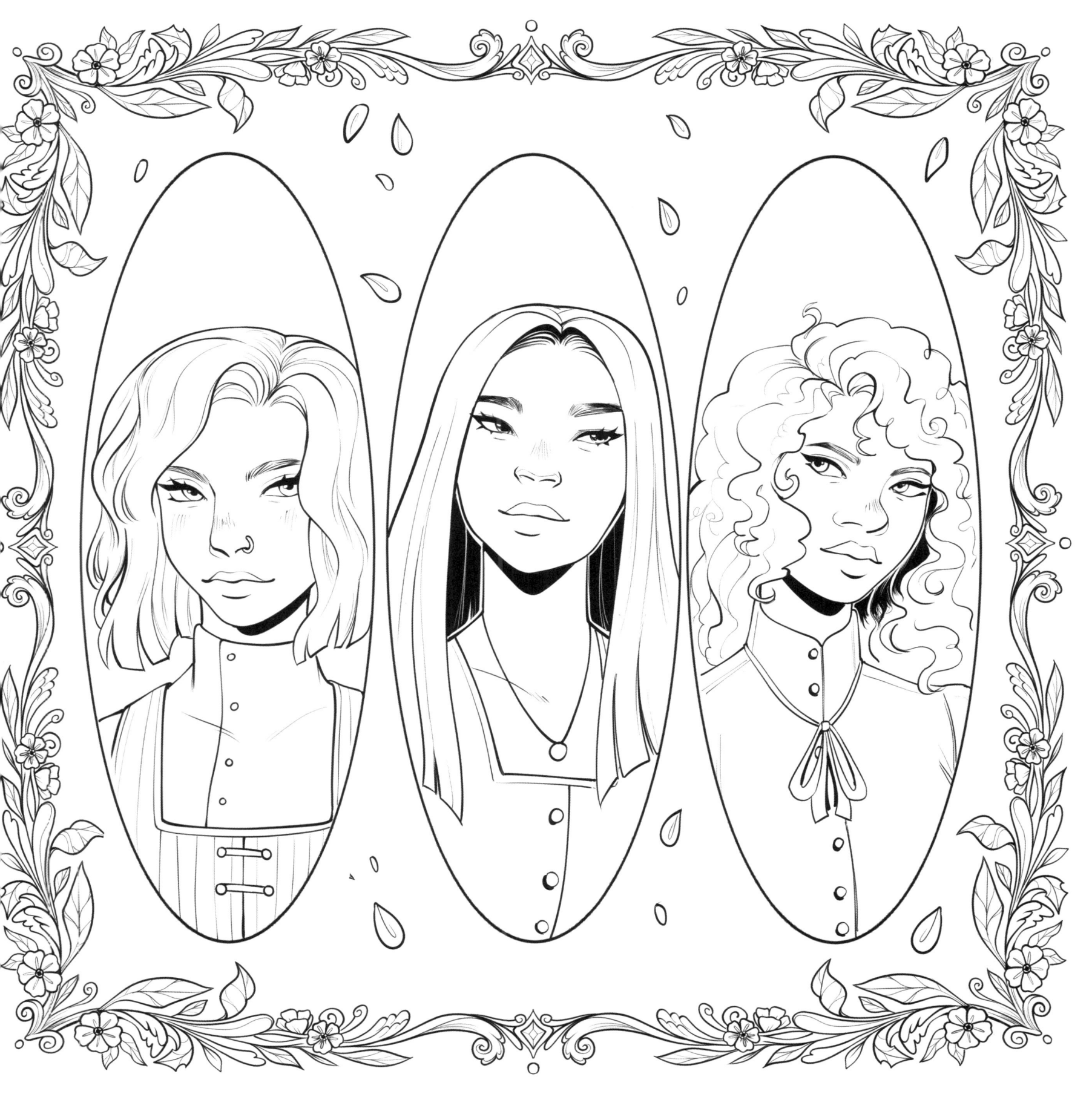

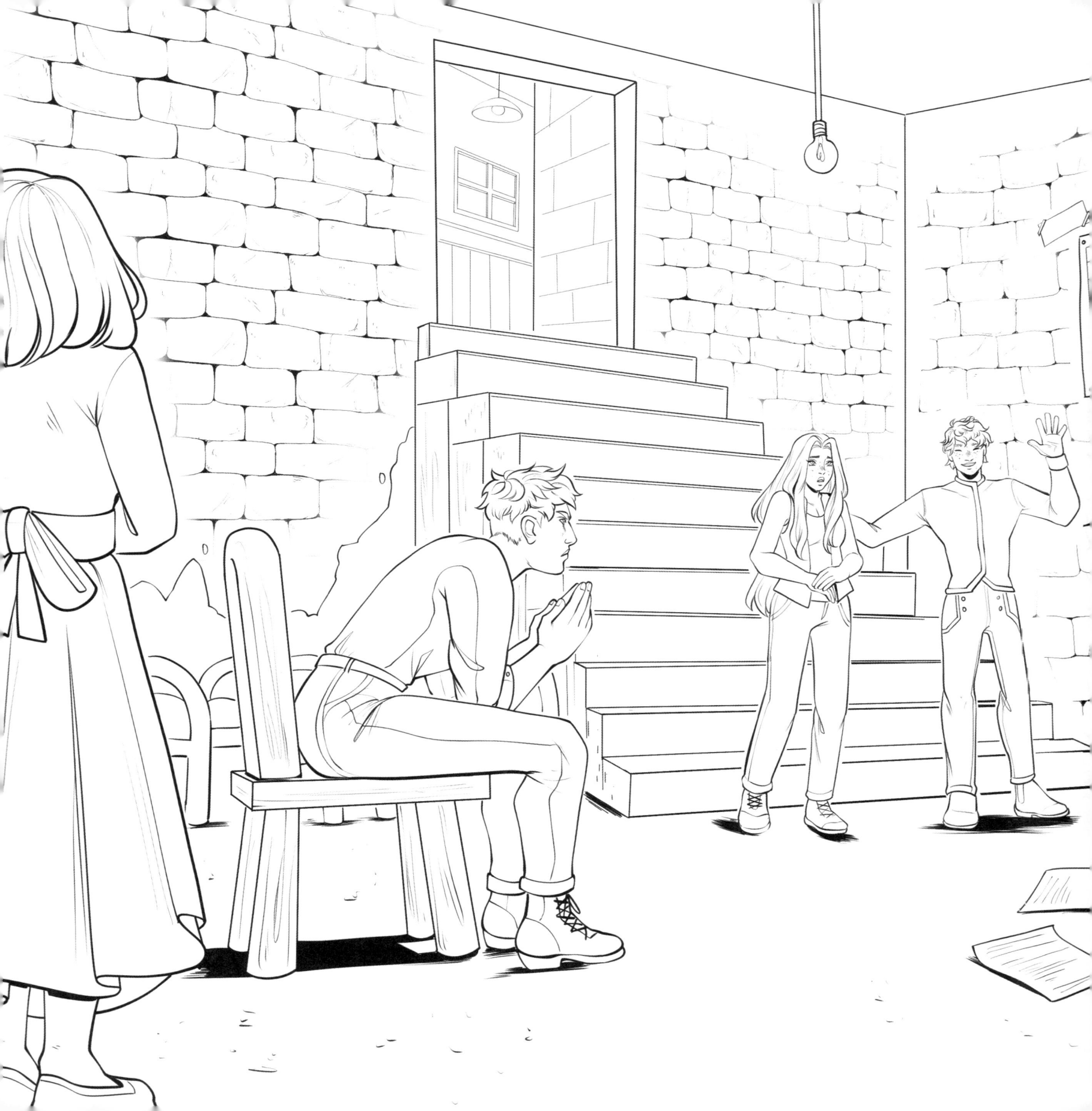

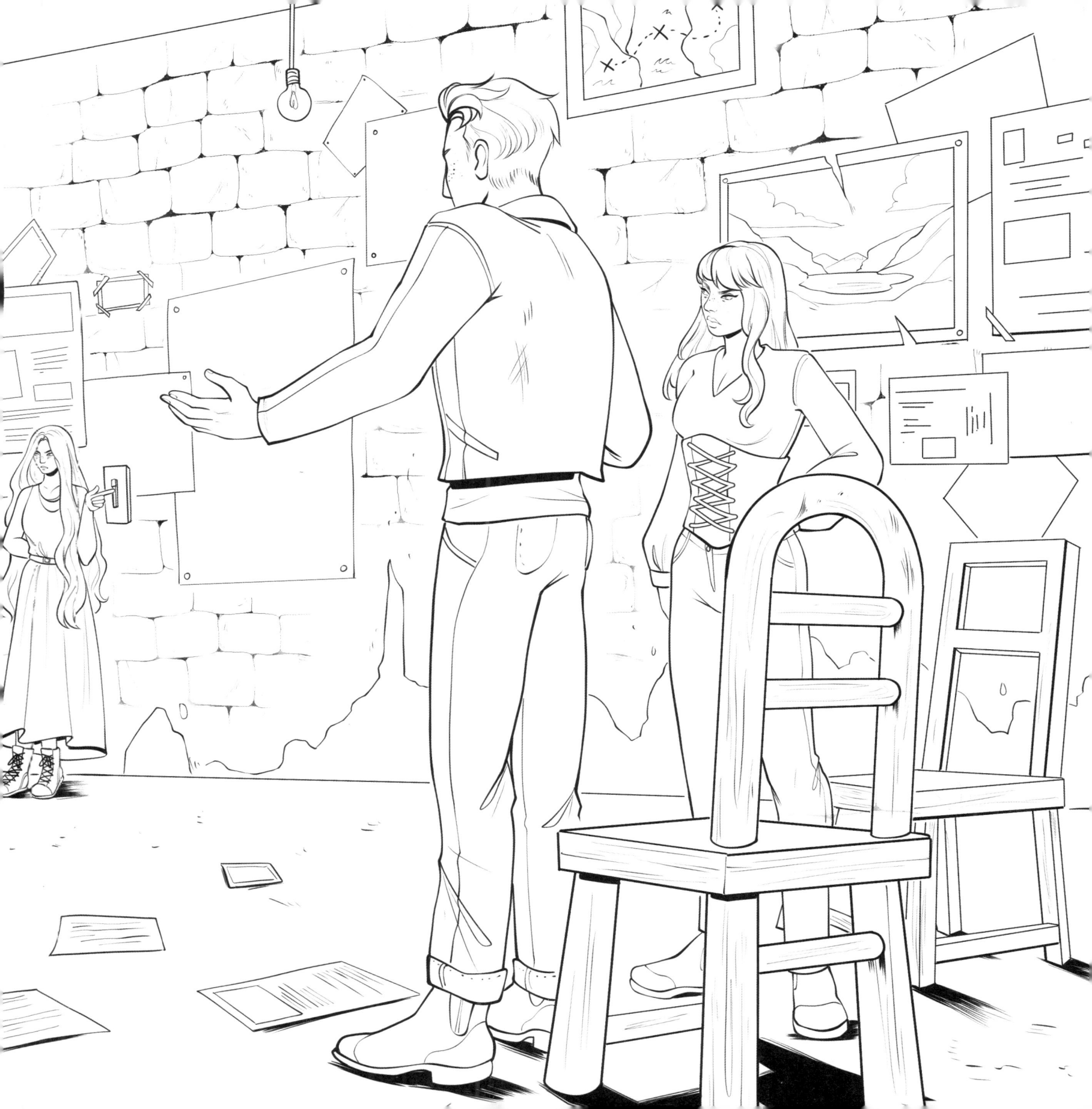

I turn toward Kitt and force out a laugh. "Don't you ever just need a break from the chaos of the castle?" Even as I say it, I already know the answer. He practically admitted to feeling trapped in the palace, in his position, when we were stuffed in the safe room together. And yet, here I am, using that information he trusted me with against him.

He looks at me, eyes seeming to search mine with a certain sadness. "You have no idea."

I throw my arms out, exasperated. "So, why don't you? You could visit Loot for a day. Granted, there's just as much chaos there as in the castle, but . . . it's a different kind of chaos. You blend in. Let the chaos wash over you until it's a familiar feeling. Until you become a part of it, swallowed in it."

Come on. Say yes.

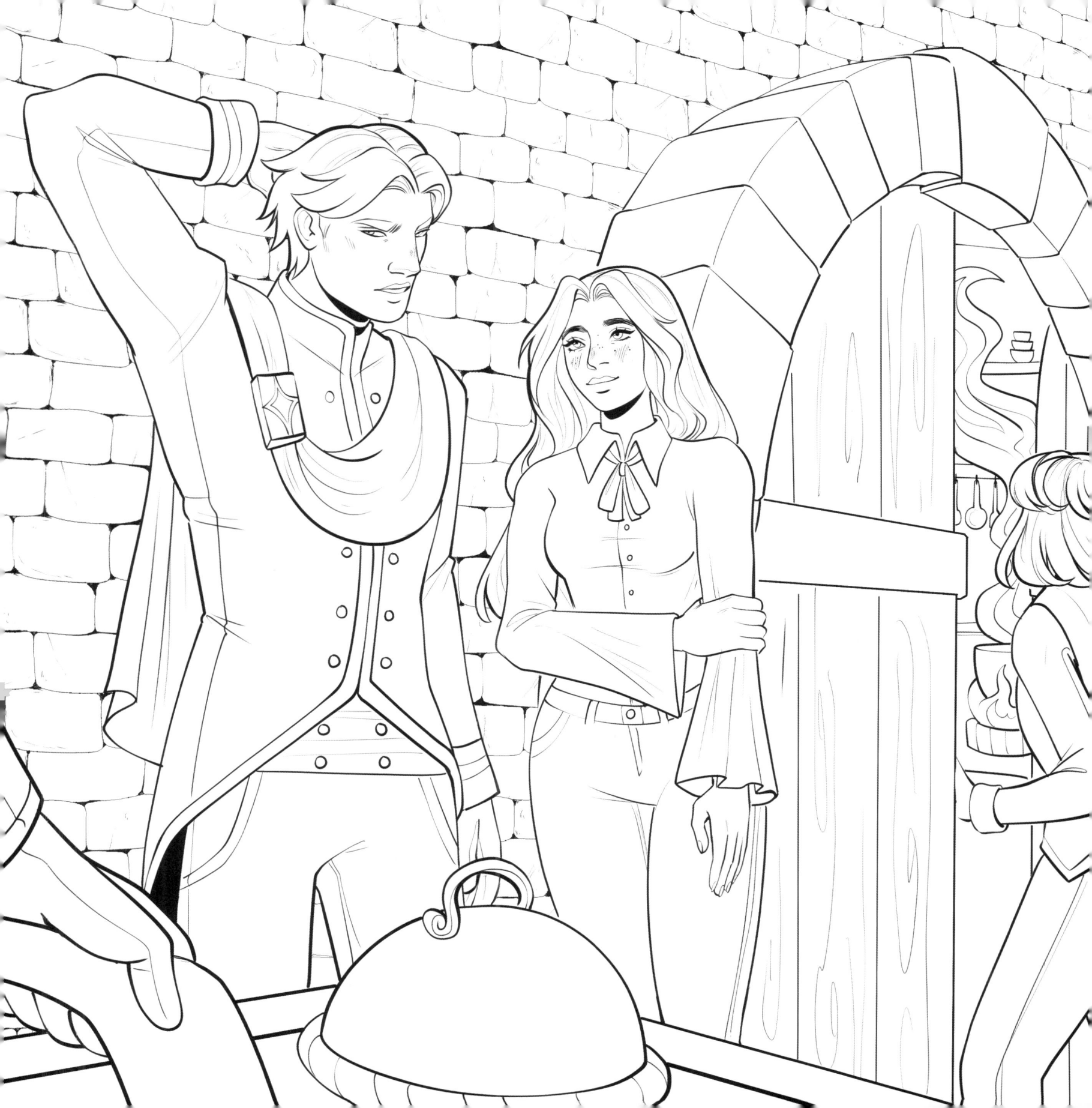

"I doubt I need to remind you of your place, so stay out of their way and we won't have any problems. Understood?"

The dagger tucked into my boot has never tempted me more, tormenting me with the thought of shoving its blade through his chest like he did to my father. But he didn't just kill my only parent that day— he killed a piece of me in the process.

And I have never hated someone so wholeheartedly because of it.

My fists are clenched tightly at my sides, fingernails biting into my palms. But I school my face into a submissive, sweet expression when I say, "Understood, Your Majesty."

If I didn't want to win before, I certainly do now.

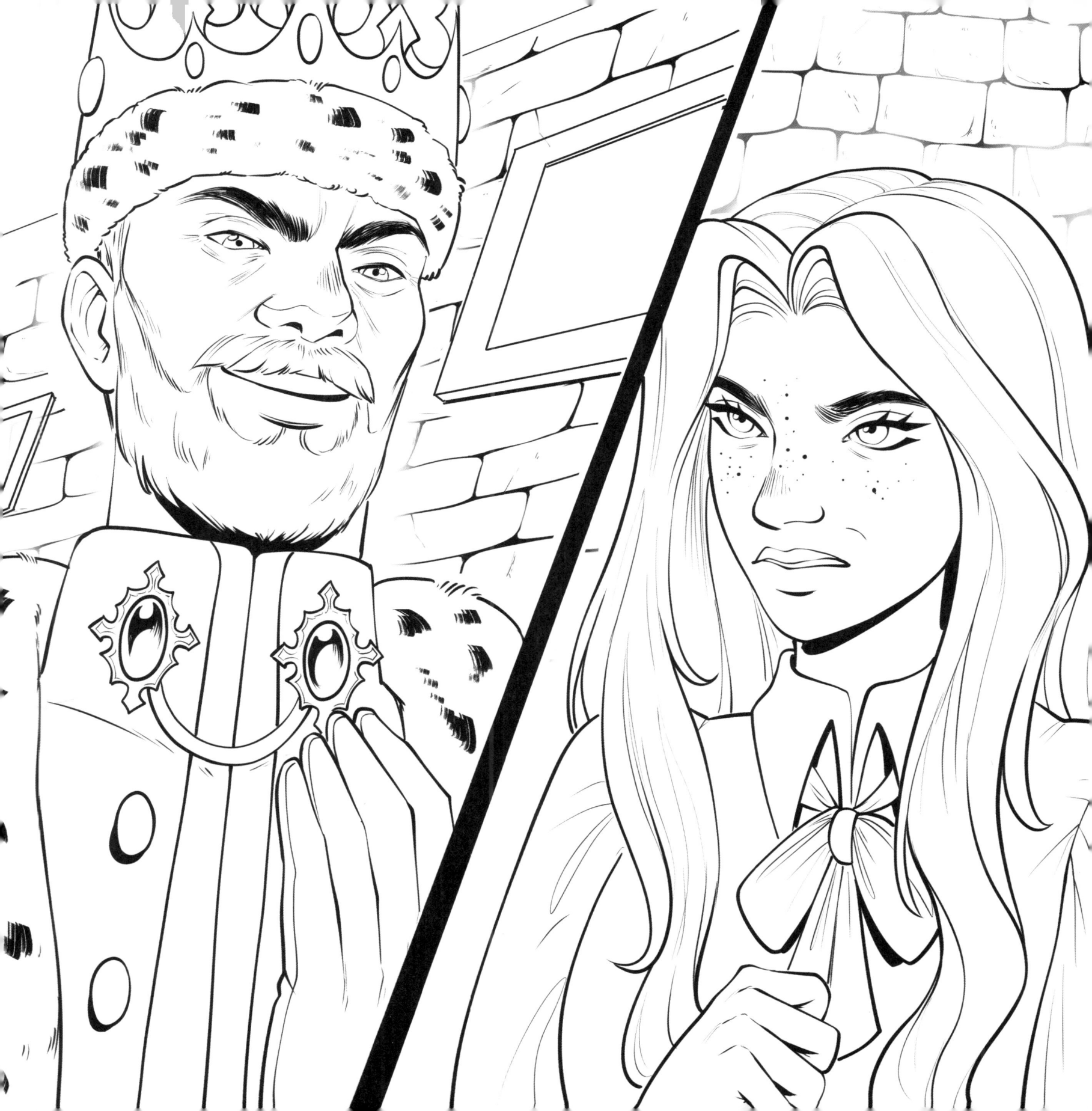

"Adena, I love it . . ." I trail off while my eyes trail over the fabric hugging my body. Then my gaze meets the excited hazel one in the mirror, and I turn to face my best friend. "I love you, Adena."

She glows, beaming at me brightly. "And I love you, Pae." Her smile turns sly. "And *everyone* is going to love you in this dress. Especially a certain prince . . ."

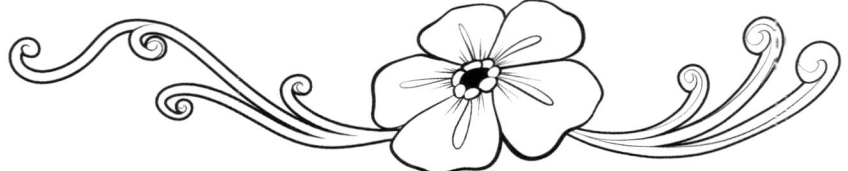

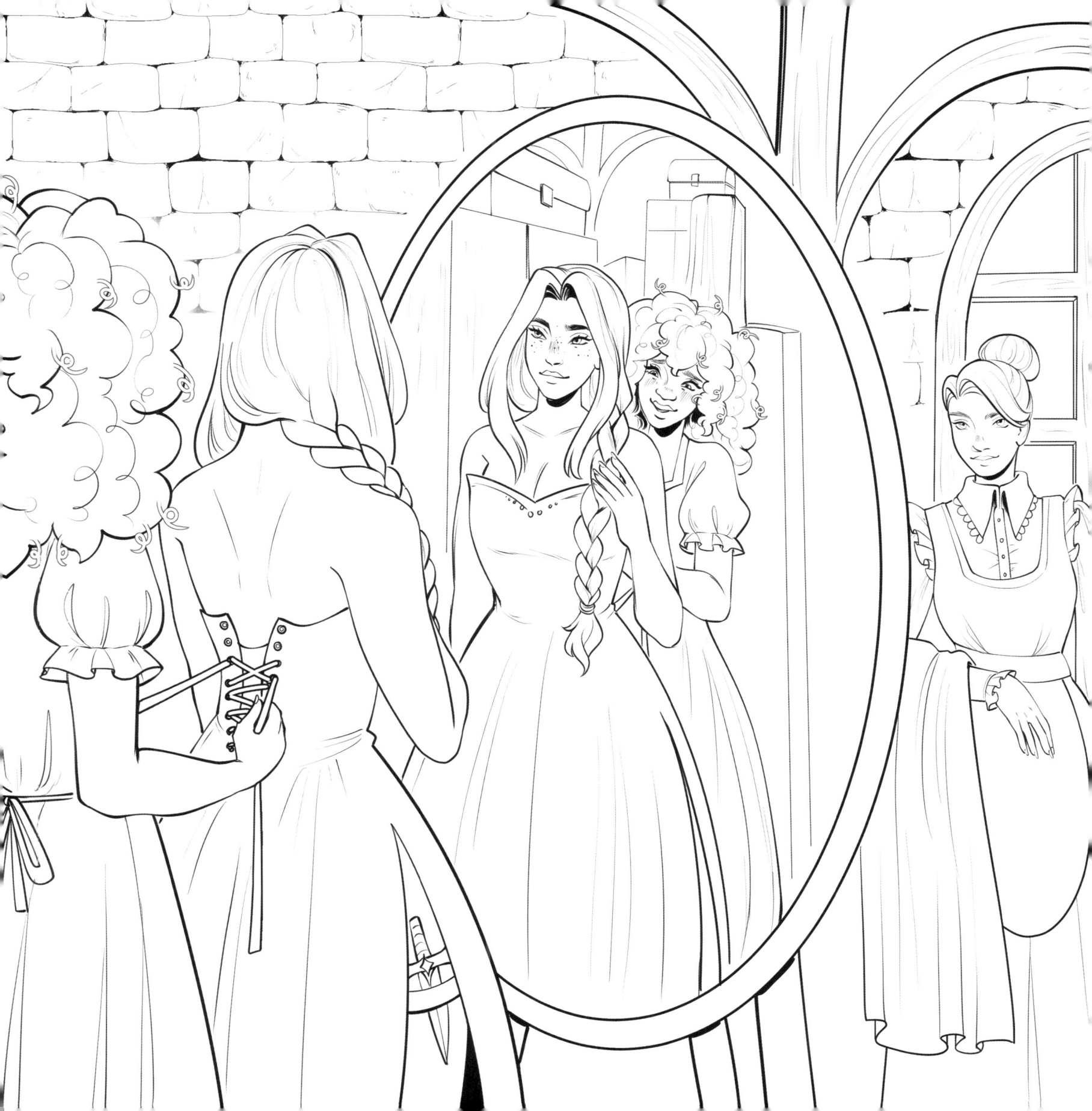

ACE ELWAY

STATUS: ELITE

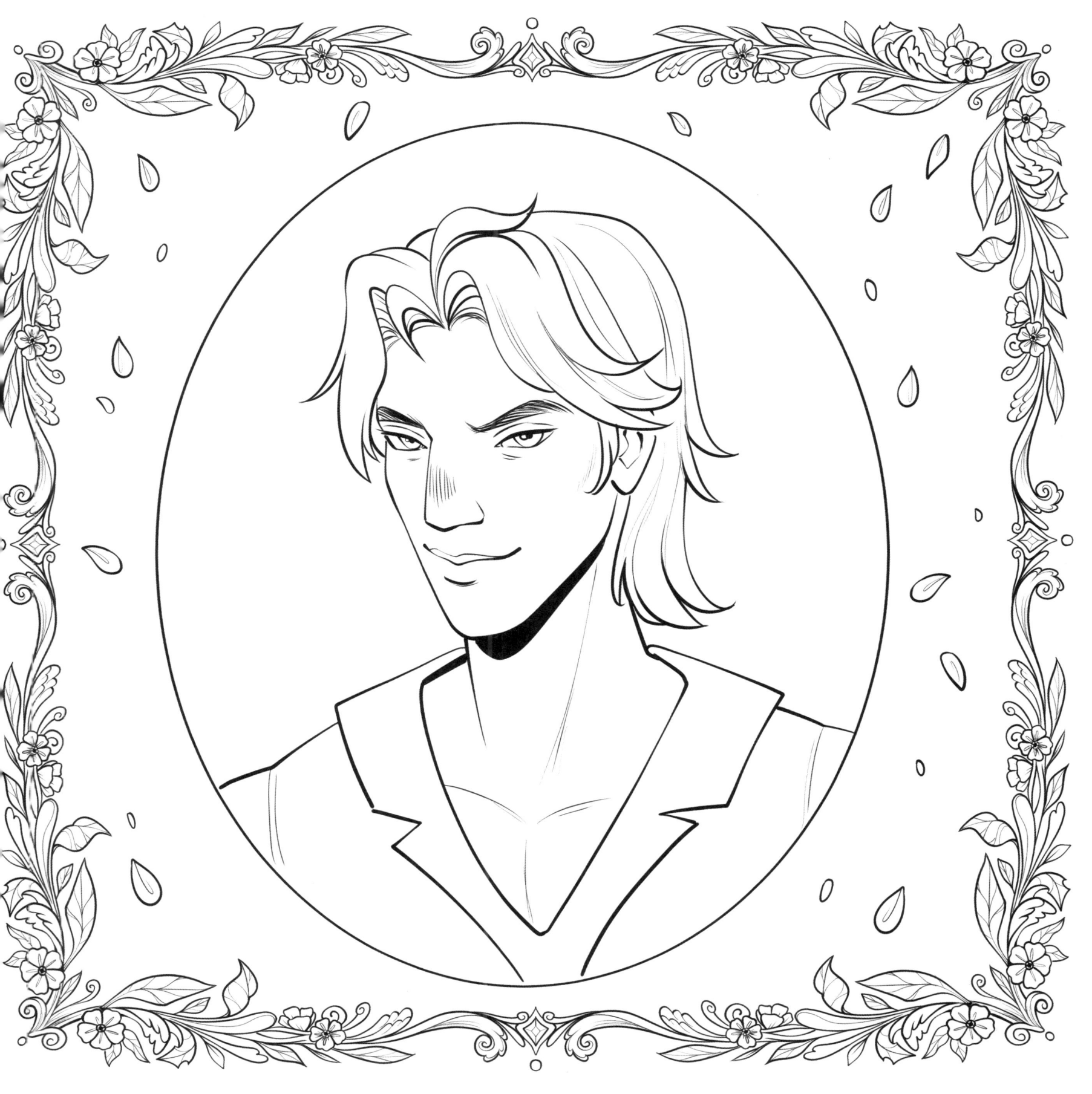

I blink, trying to clear my head as I turn and step into the ring.

My eyes scan over the crowd, stopping only when they meet the king's from where he is sitting in a carved wooden chair beside his queen. I don't think I imagine the flicker of smug satisfaction that crosses his face, making me wonder just how *random* these pairings truly are. It wouldn't surprise me in the slightest if this were the king's doing, wanting to see Blair tear me apart just as much as the people likely do.

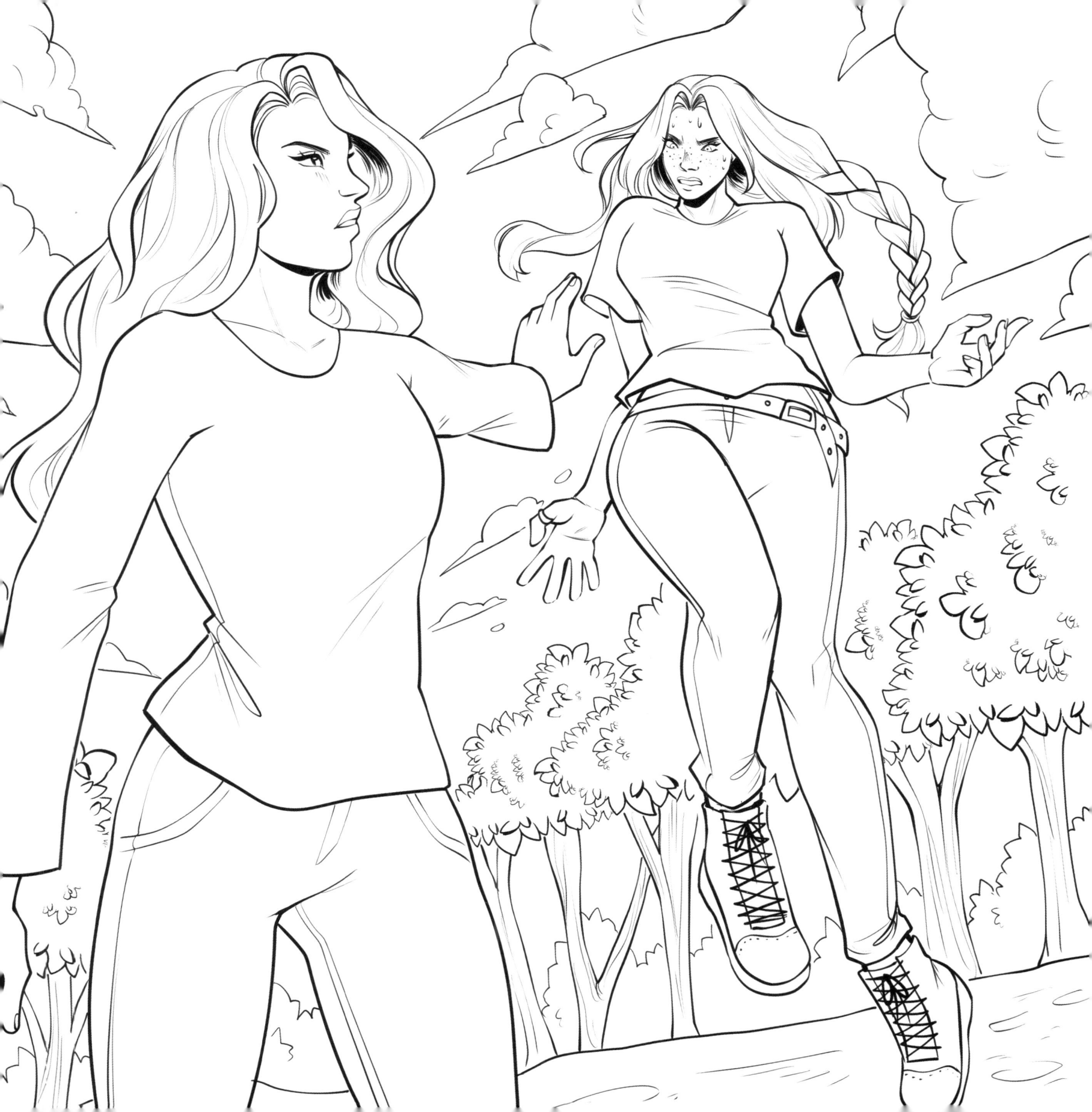

"Kai." Her voice is little more than a whisper. "Don't. Move."

I follow her gaze to where dozens of beady, black eyes stare back at me, forked tongues flicking. Snakes. Huge and hungry. I can't even make out how many of them there are with all the underbrush and rocks scattering the ground, but I know that there are enough for me to be worried.

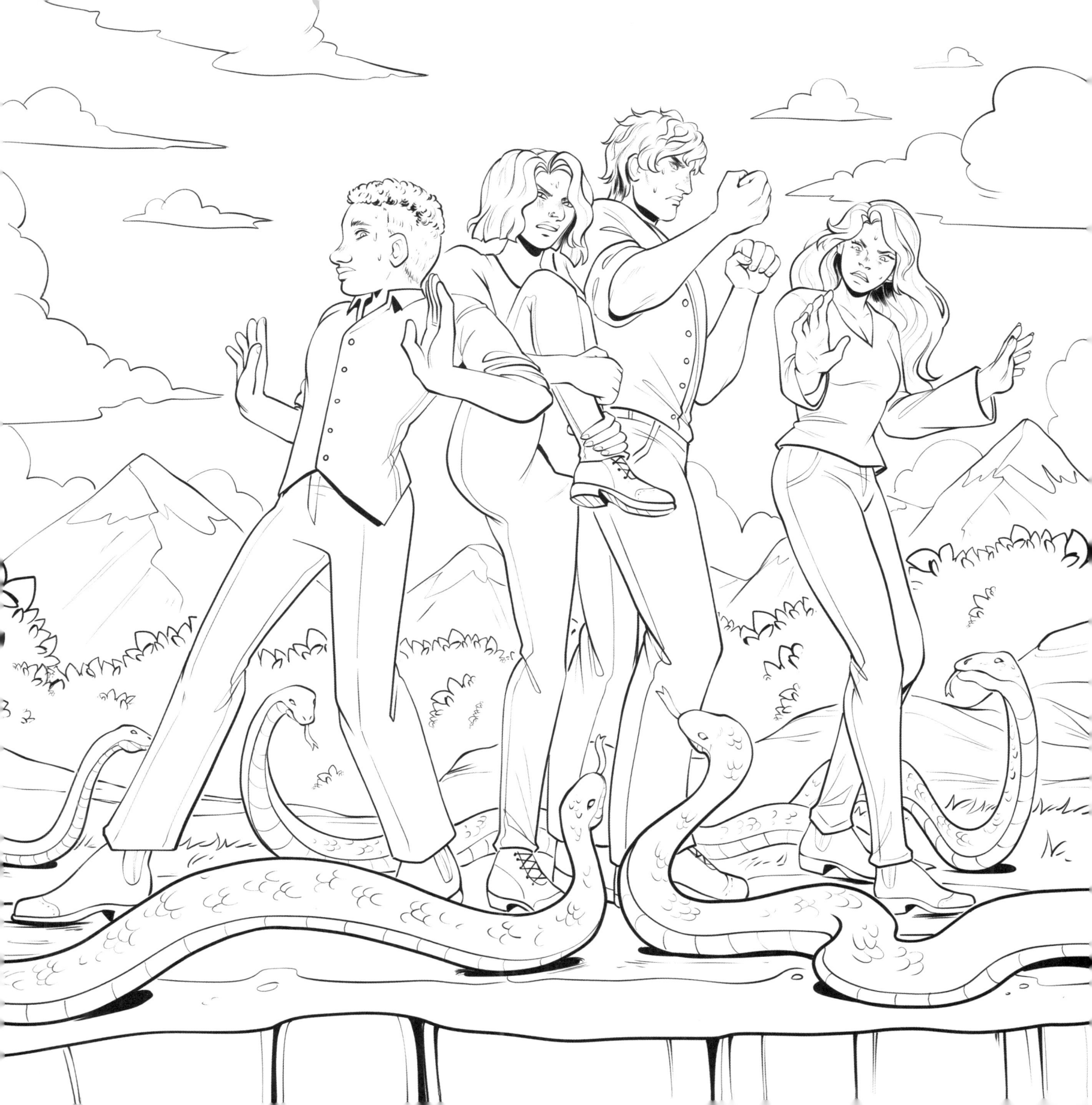

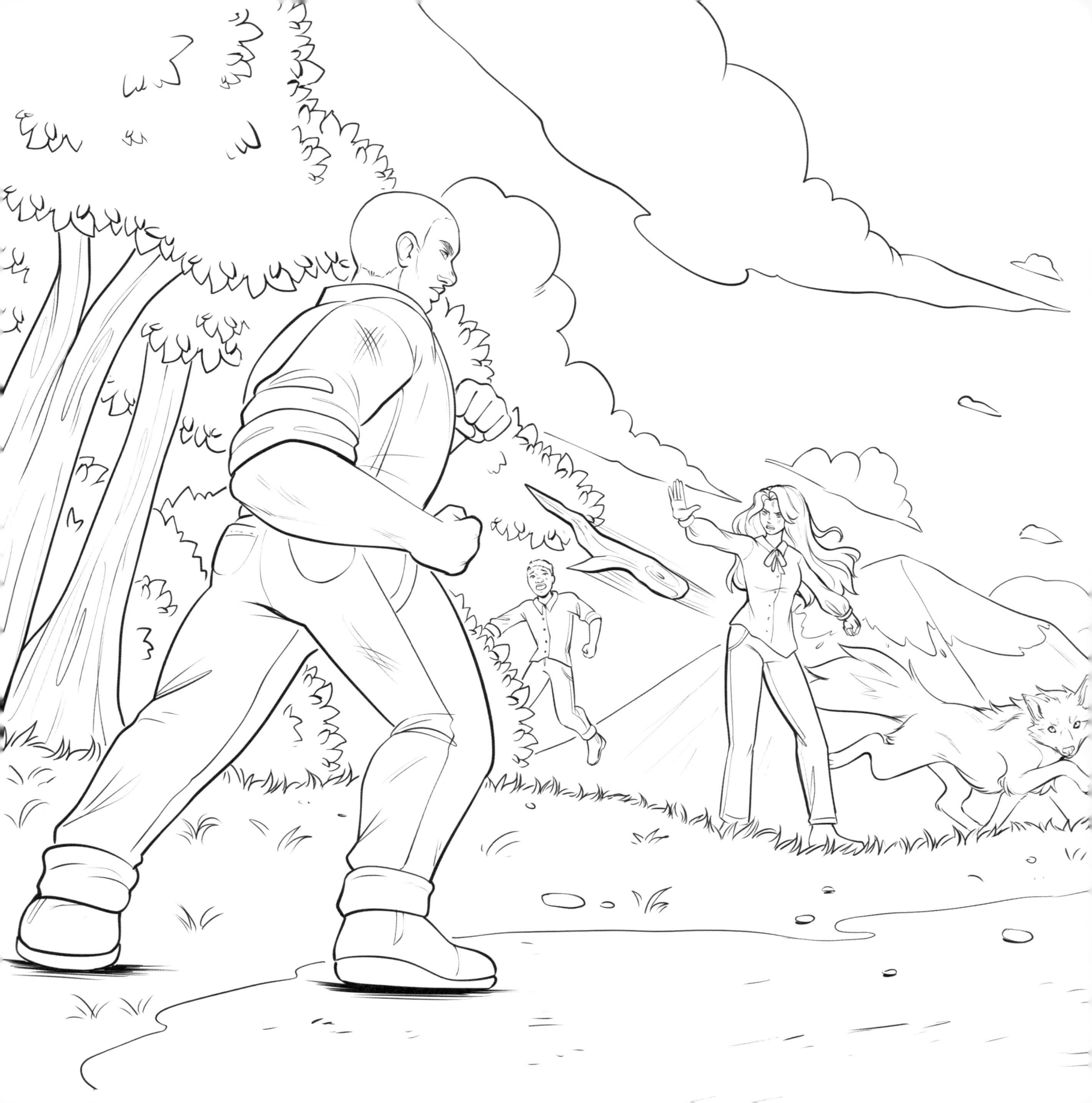

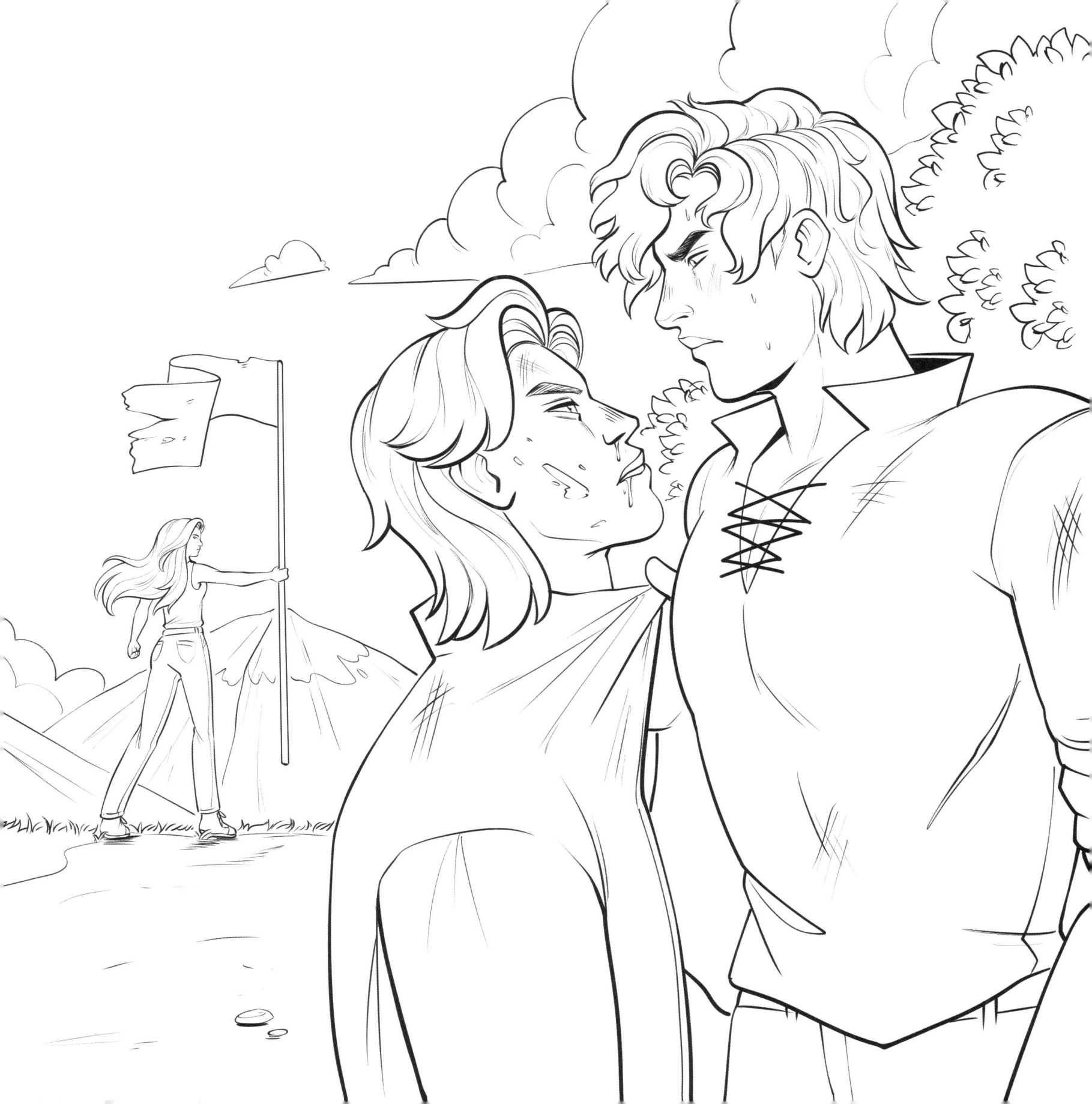

"So why are you here?"

I smile slightly and echo his words. "To think. I like the quiet. The escape."

I see his lips twitch out of the corner of my eye, and we are quiet for a moment before I ask, "Is there a reason you dragged me down onto the dirt?"

I look over at his shadowy profile as he stares at the branches above us. "To talk. To lie here in silence." He shrugs lazily. "It doesn't really matter."

I look away from him. "So, you just want someone to keep you company?"

"Not someone. You."

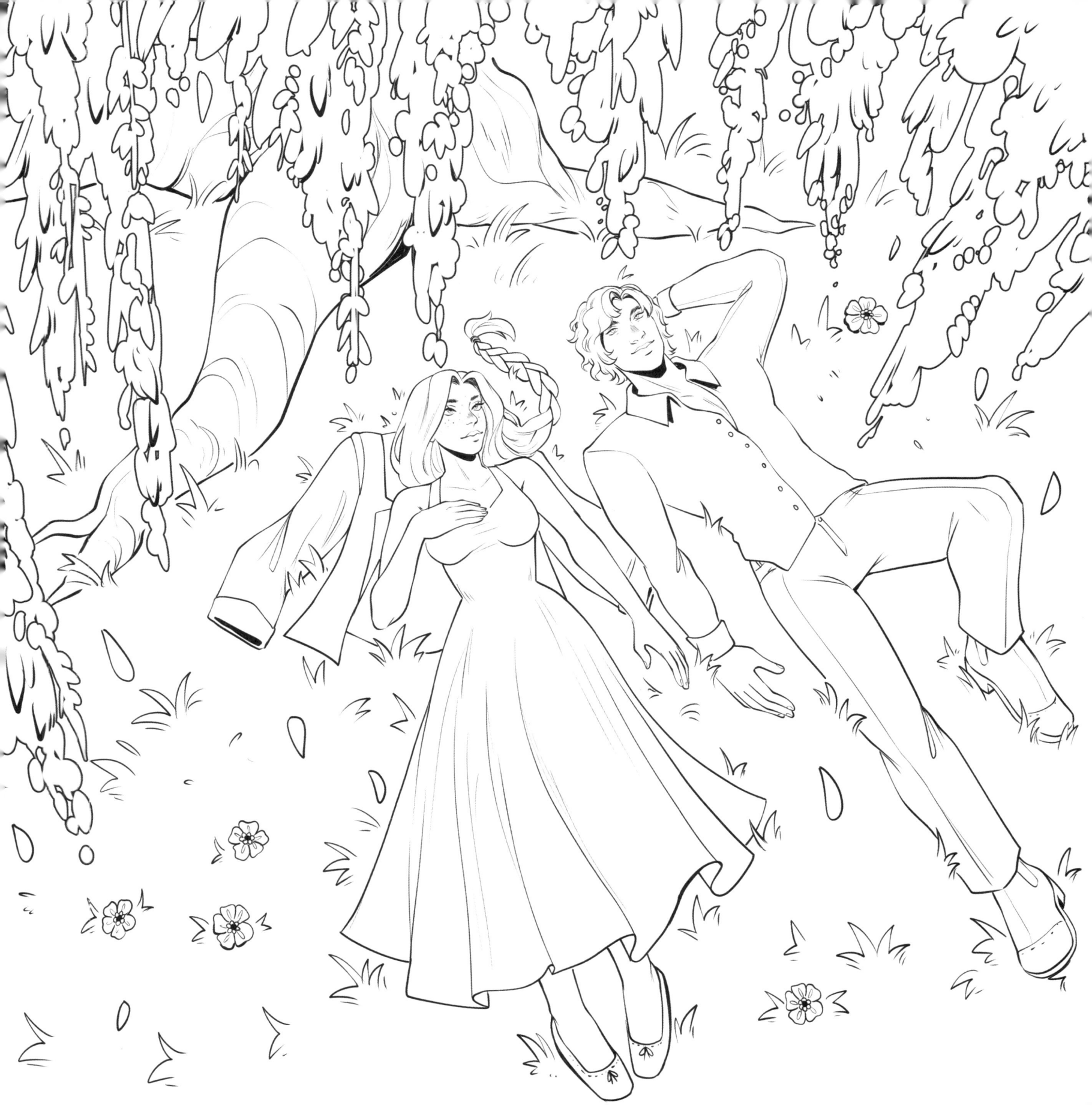

BRAXTON HALE

STATUS: ELITE

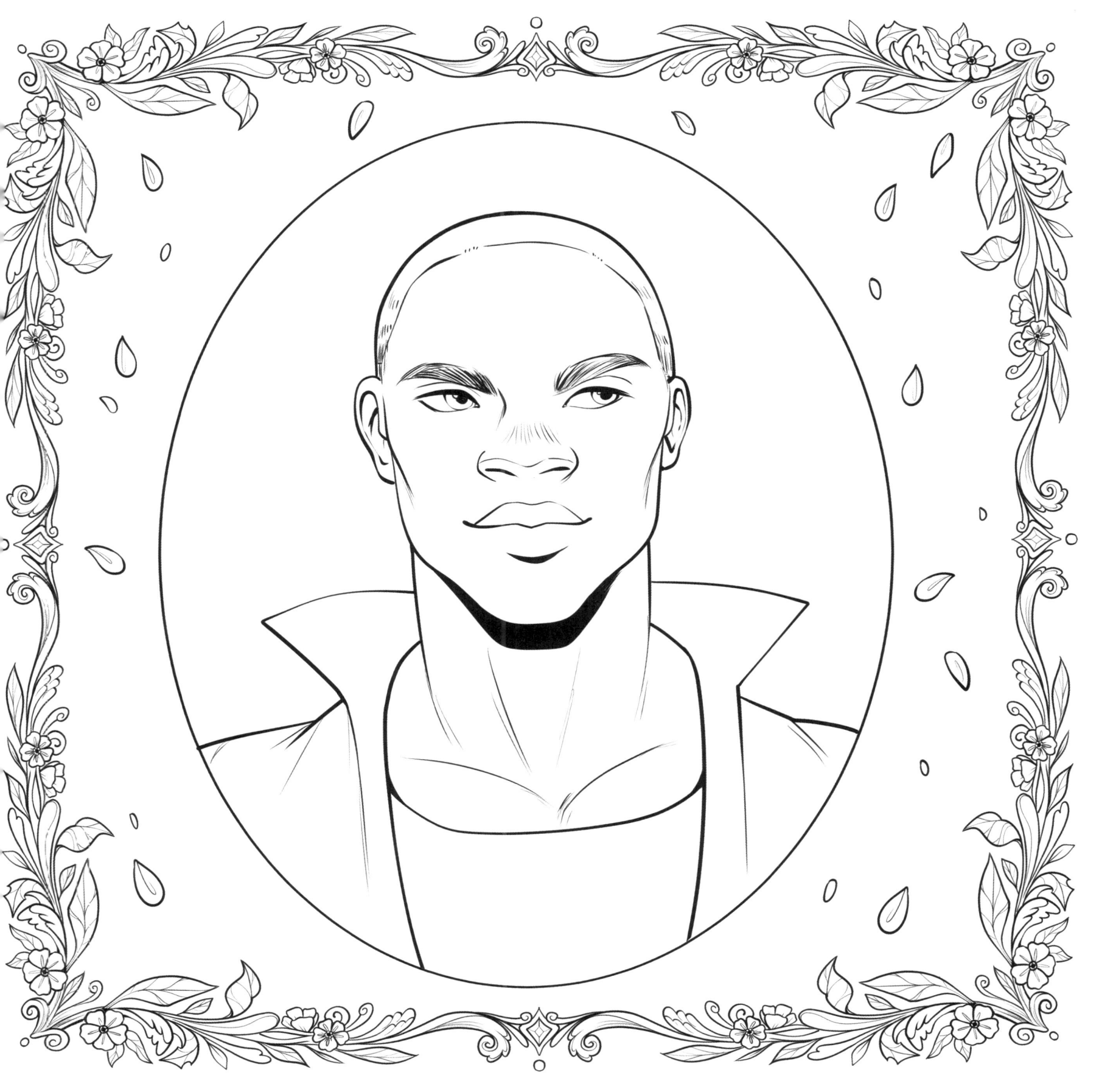

"In here," Kitt says, snapping my attention back to the task at hand.

His head sweeps back and forth down the hallway, and after deeming the coast clear, we step into the last cell.

My heart leaps into my throat, and I swallow. The passage is in a *cell*. It's brilliant, really. I would have never guessed that an escape out of the castle would be connected to the one place they don't want anyone to escape from.

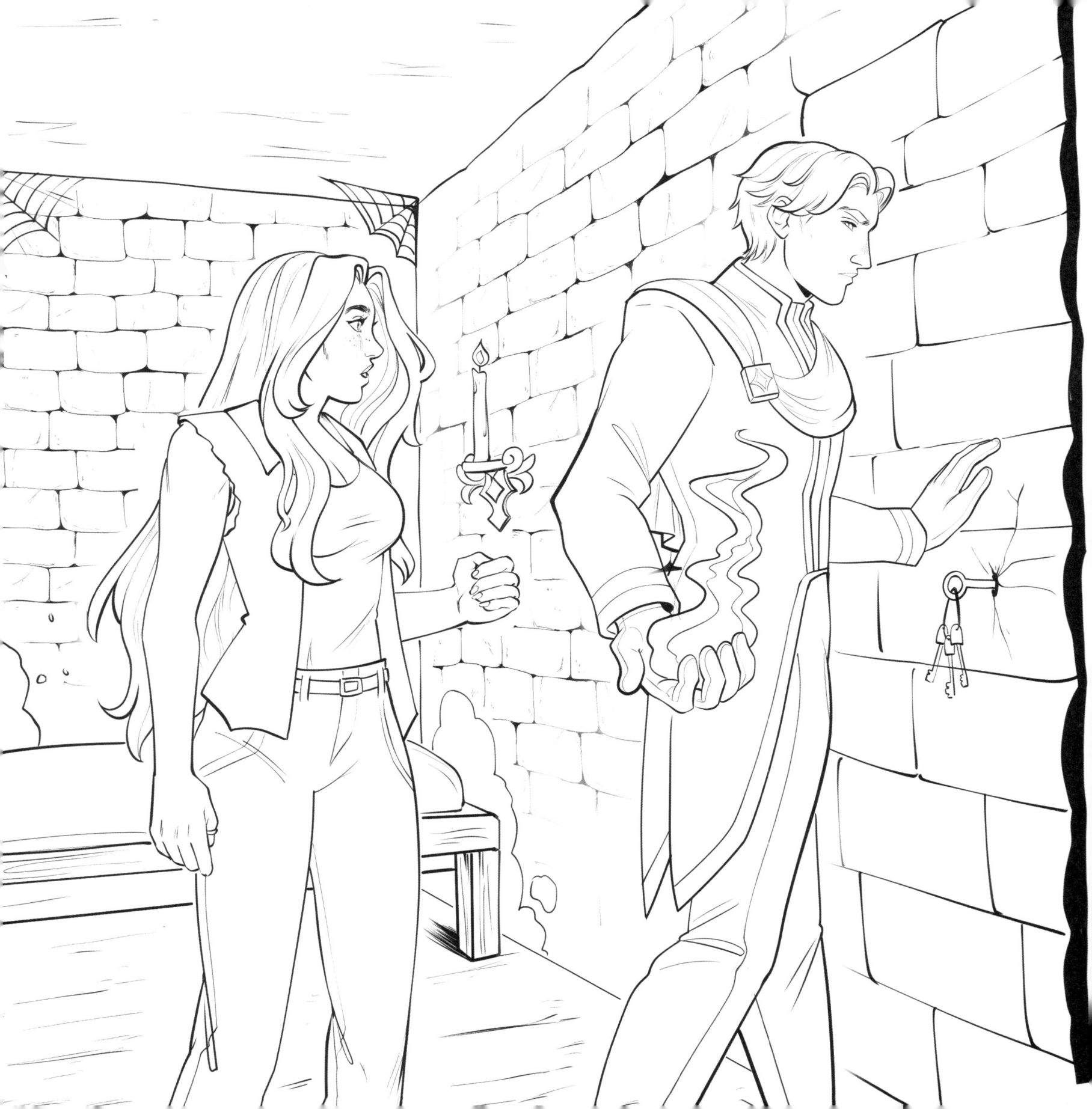

"Kai. It was just a nightmare." I keep my voice calm while ignoring my thundering heart that says I'm anything but. "Kai, it's me. Paedyn."

He blinks. And then he blinks again, over and over as if clearing his head. As if seeing me for the first time. Cool air coats my neck as he pulls the dagger away, his eyes never straying from mine.

"It's me. Pae." My voice trembles, barely more than a whisper now. "Kai?" Then my voice cracks and something seems to crack inside him as well.

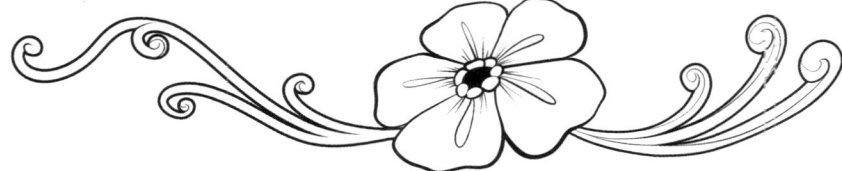

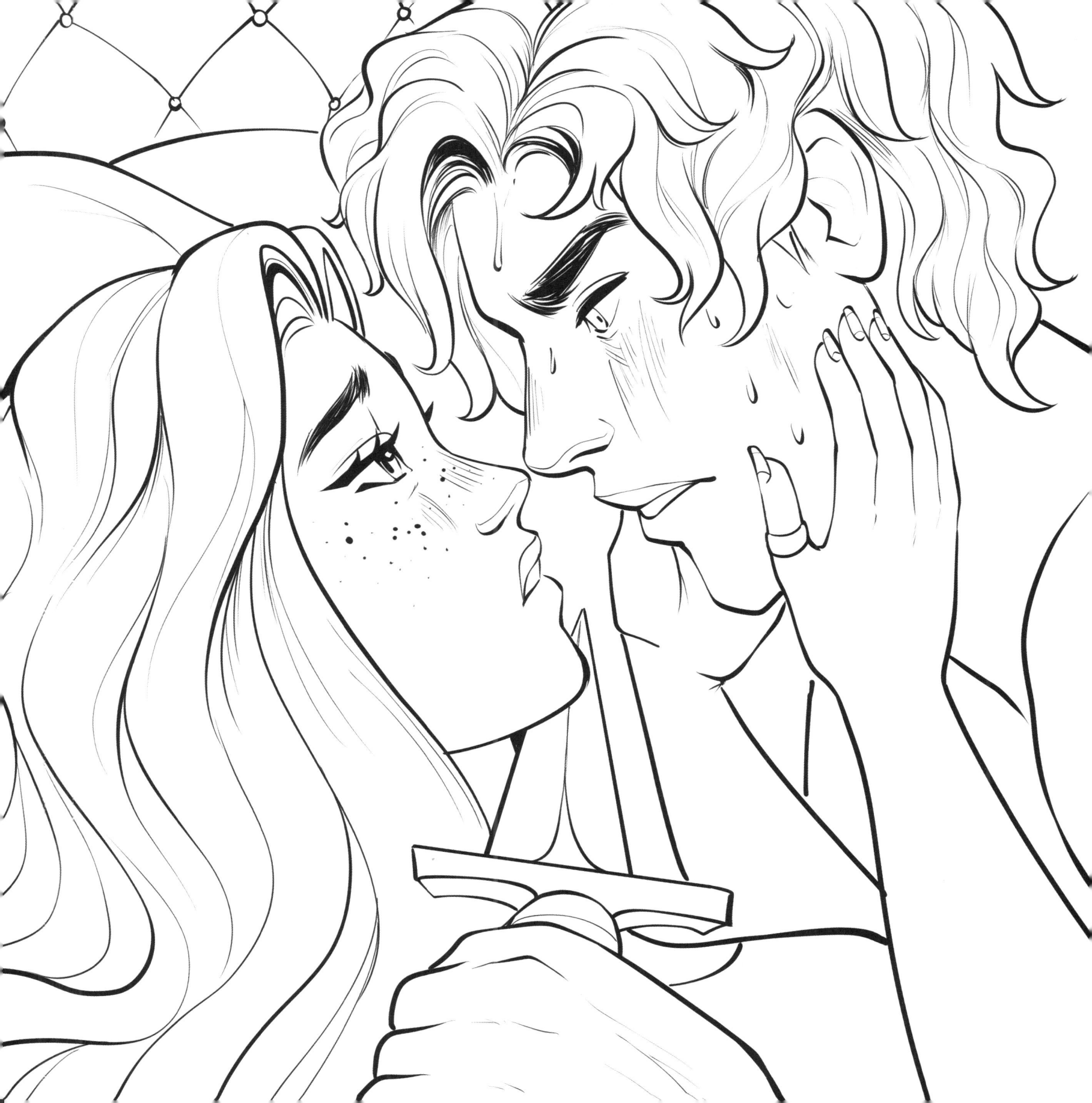

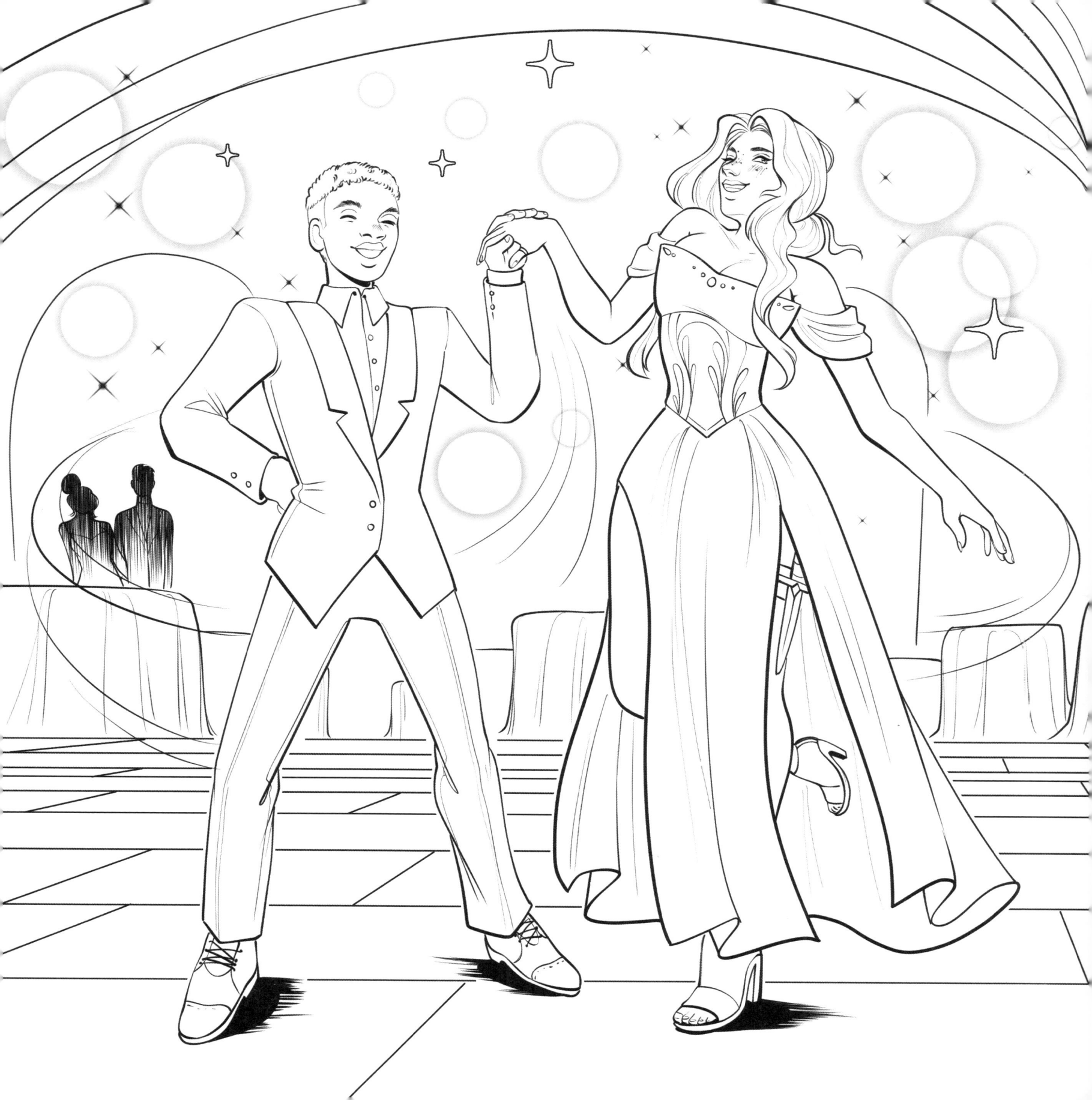

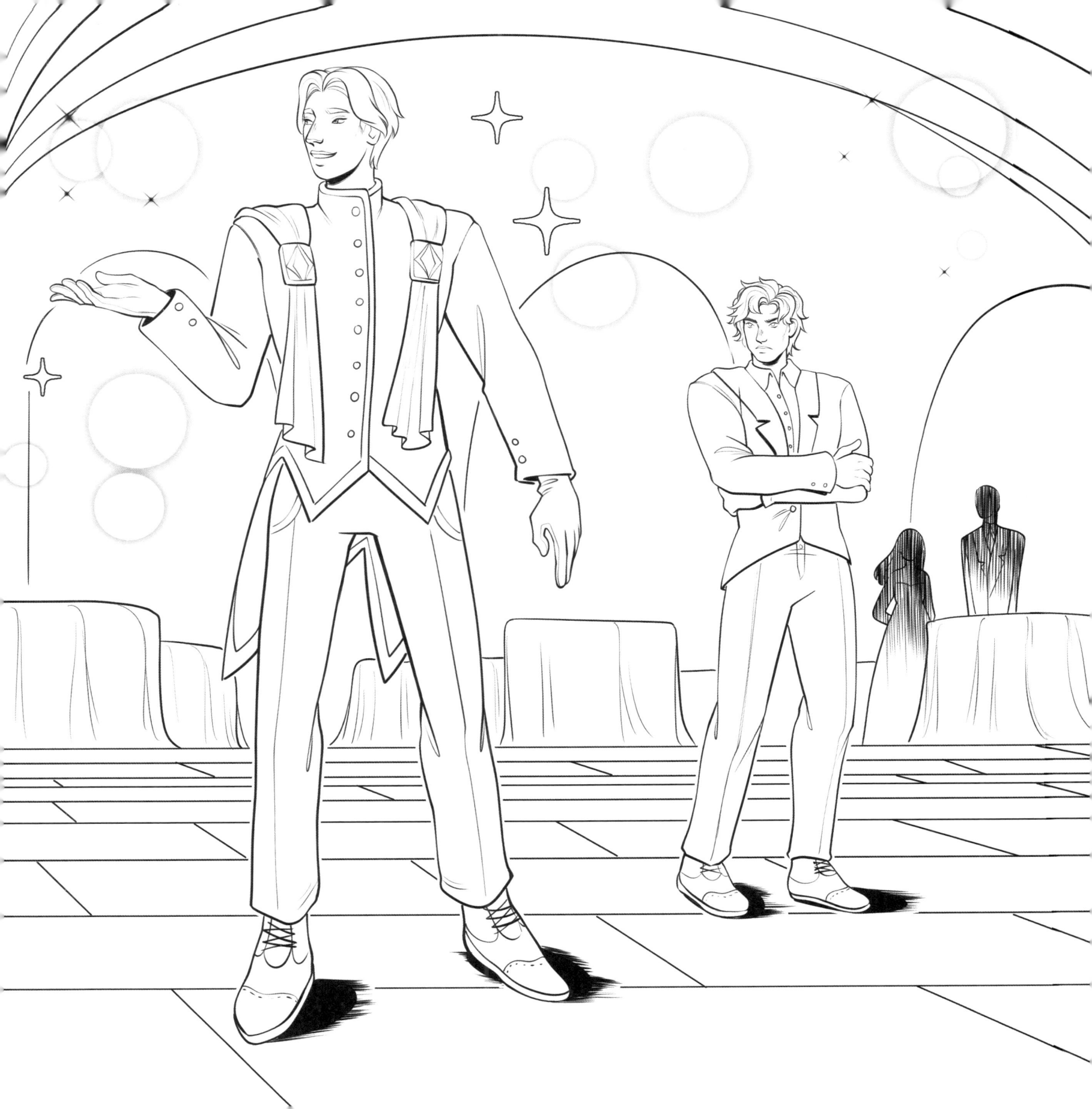

"A forget-me-not, since you always seem to be forgetting who I am," Kai says with a soft smile, a soft laugh. He lifts his hand, tucking the flower behind my ear before letting his fingers run through my wet hair.

"Oh, I know who you are," I say breathlessly. "A cocky bastard."

He shakes his head at me, his fingers still toying with strands of my hair. "I don't give a damn if you forget who I am in title, so long as you remember who I am to *you*."

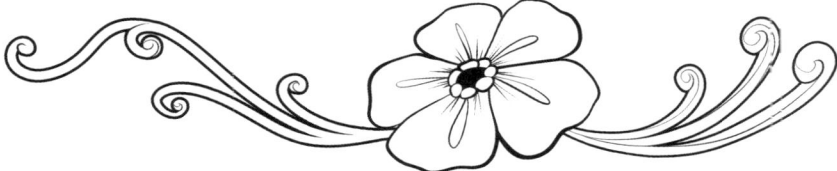

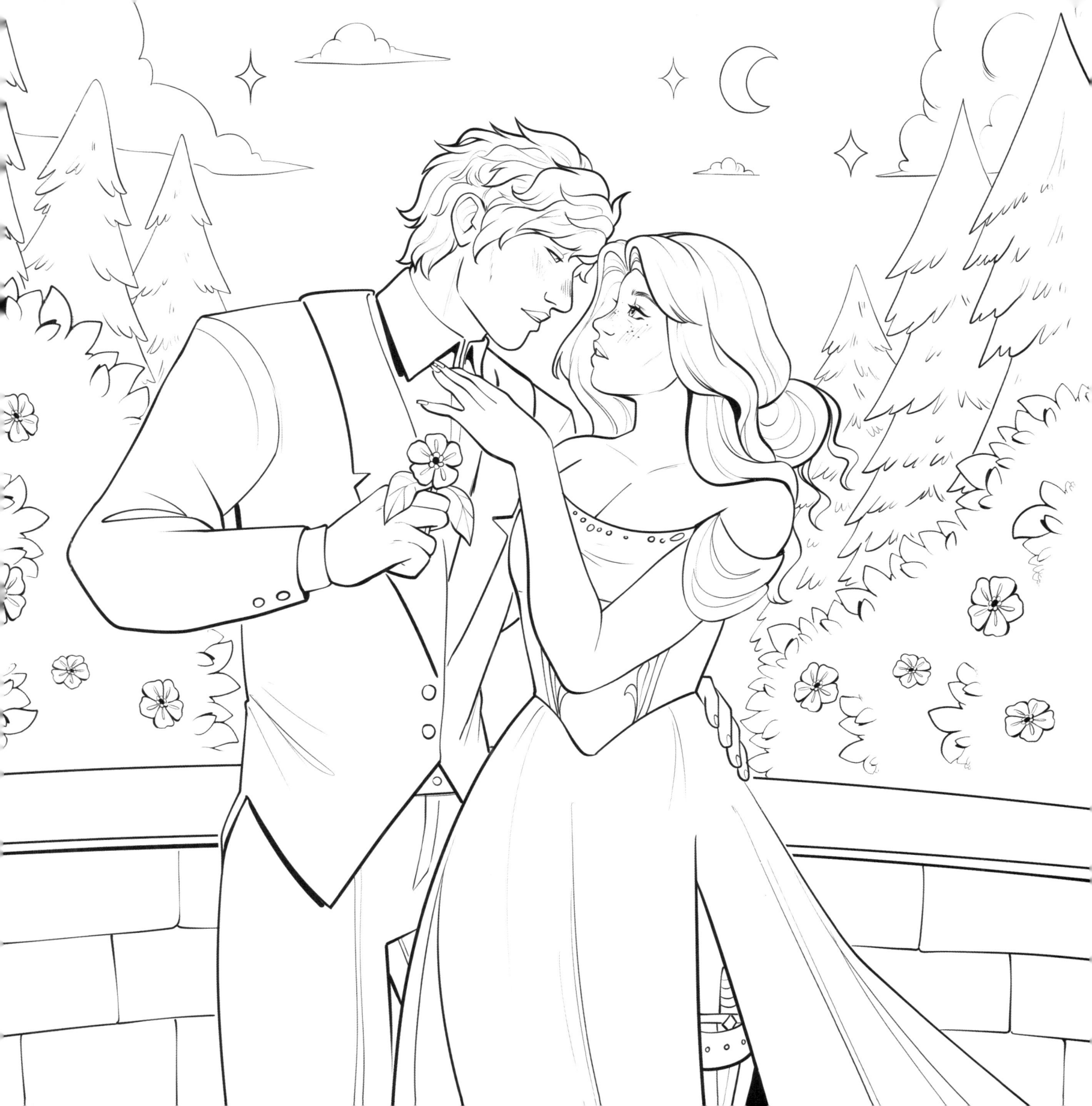

LENNY

STATUS: ELITE

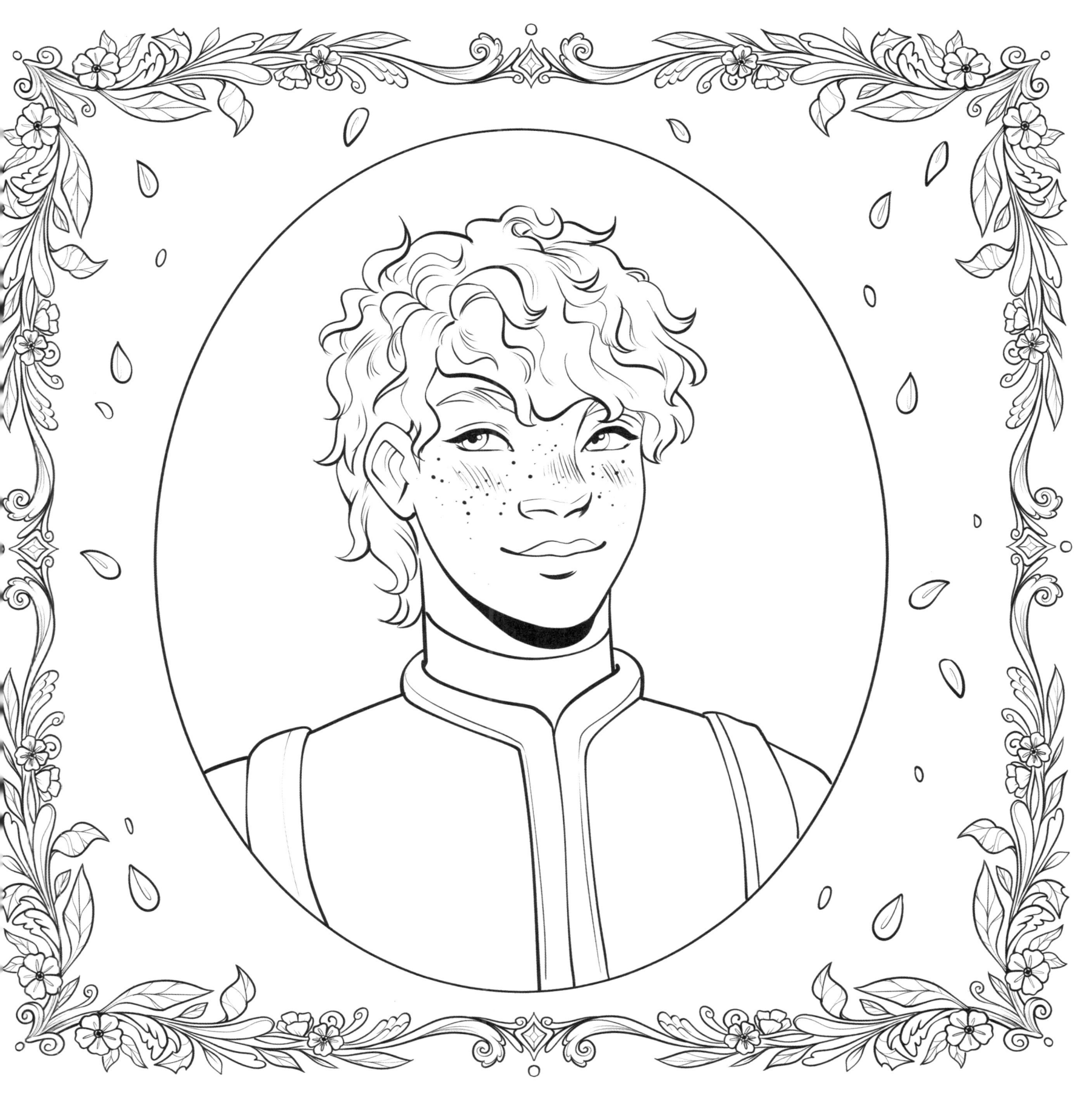

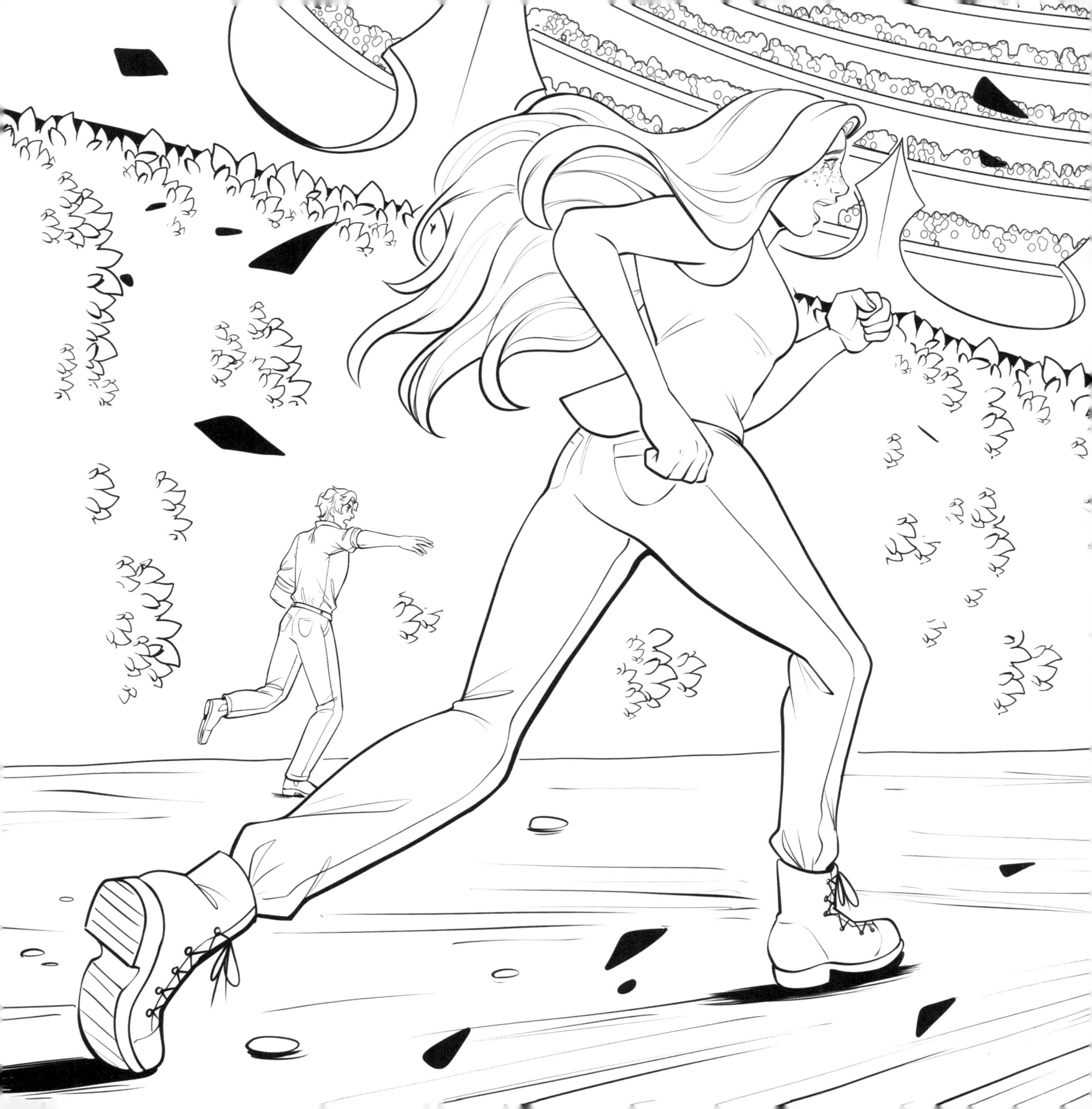

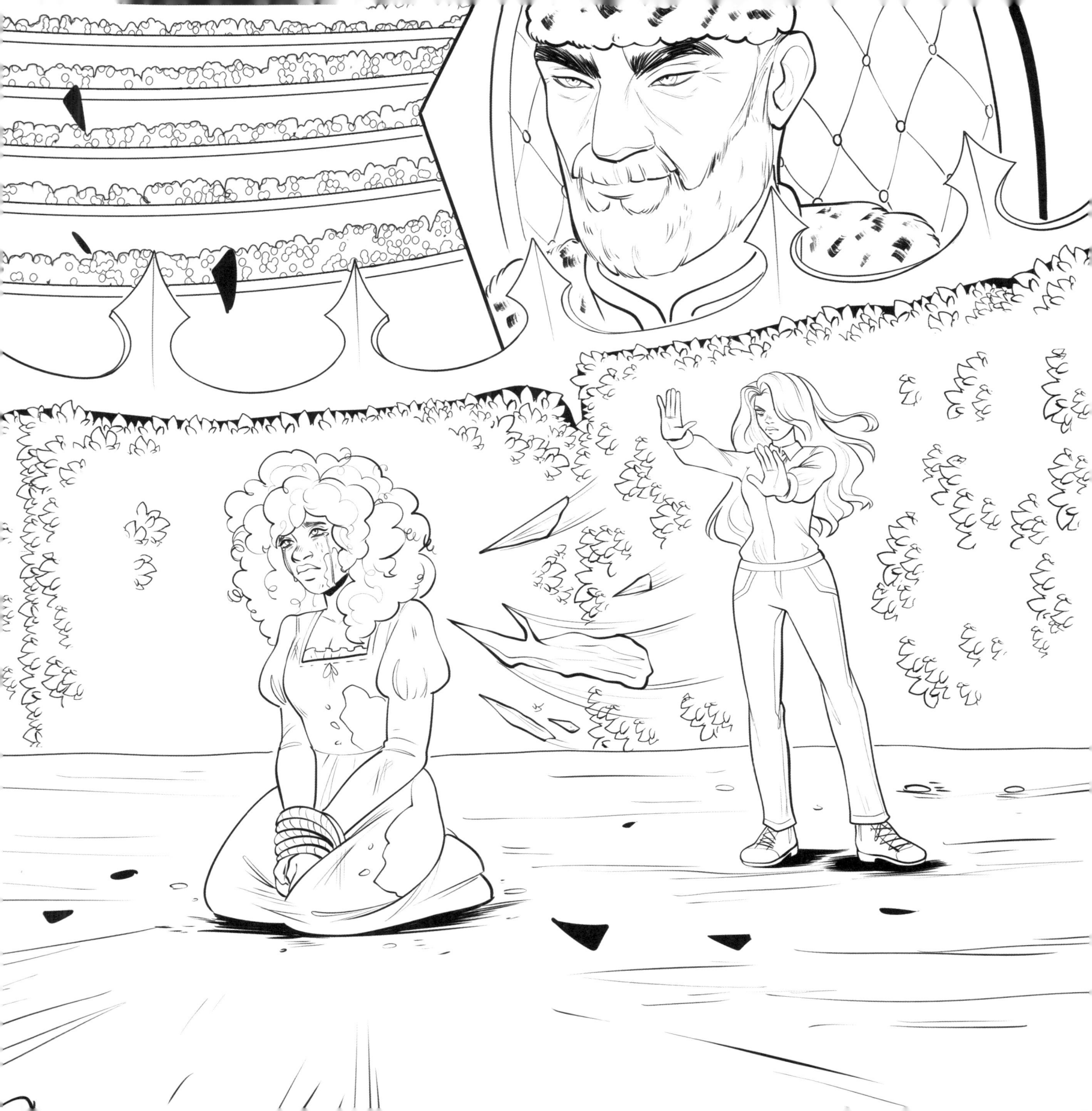

It's odd to think that the very same power the Silencer is using to suppress my ability is still my power, nonetheless.

Clinging to the Silencer's ability, feeling it flood my body, I throw it back at him.

His eyes go wide at the sudden feel of his own power battling him. He was not prepared for this, not expecting this. He let his guard down.

Only a Silencer can beat a Silencer.

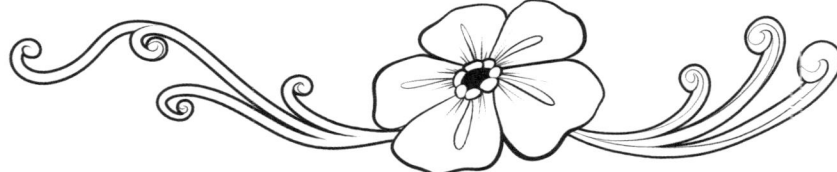

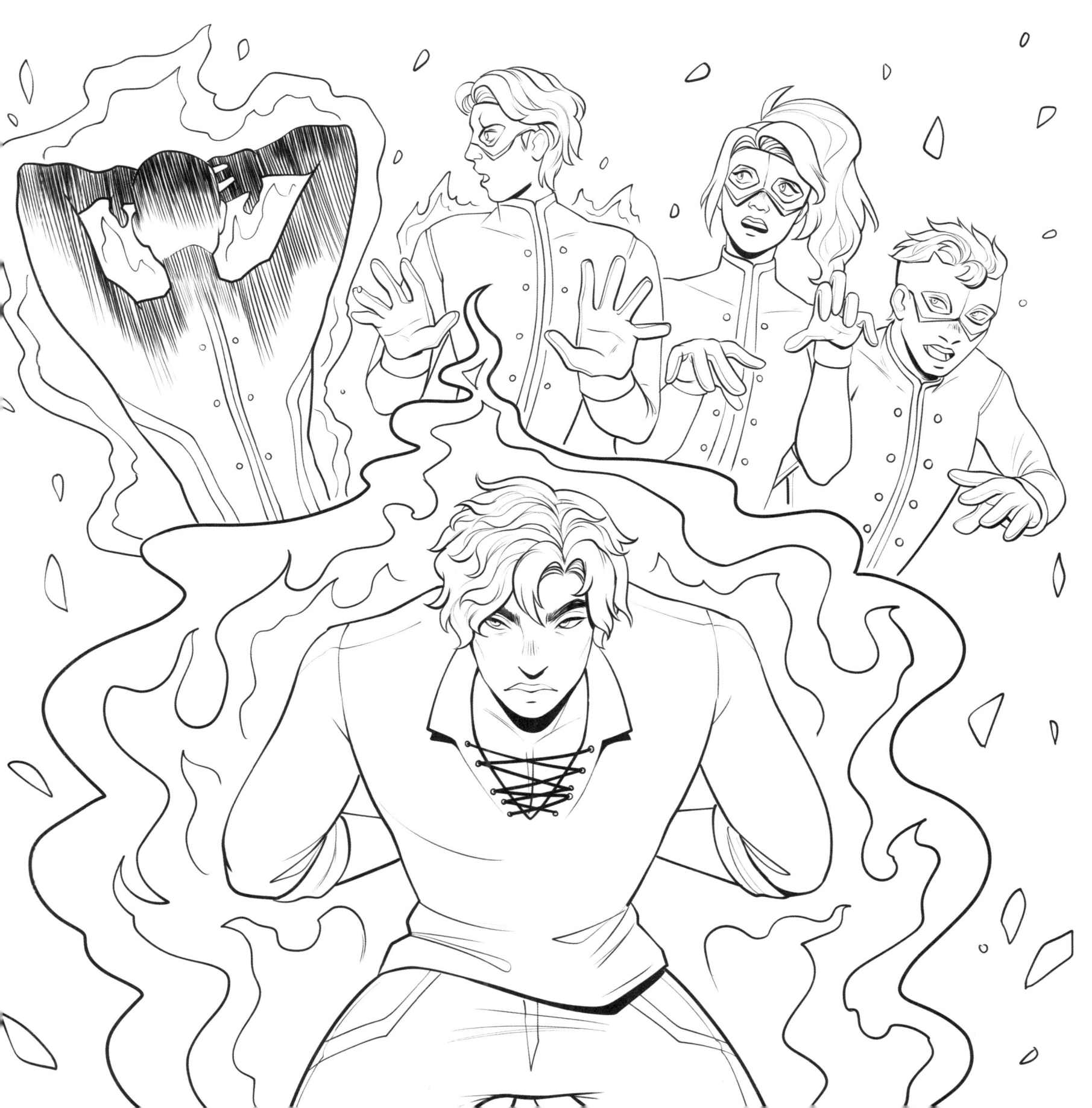

What good would you do?

Those five words snake their way into my head, wrapping around me so tightly, I feel like I might suffocate. The choking hold of that thought only tightens when nine little letters string together, creating a word equally as devastating as the last five.

Powerless.

In every sense of the word.

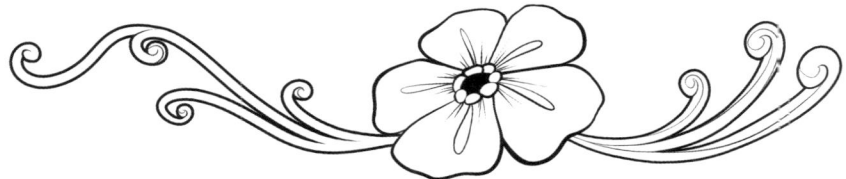

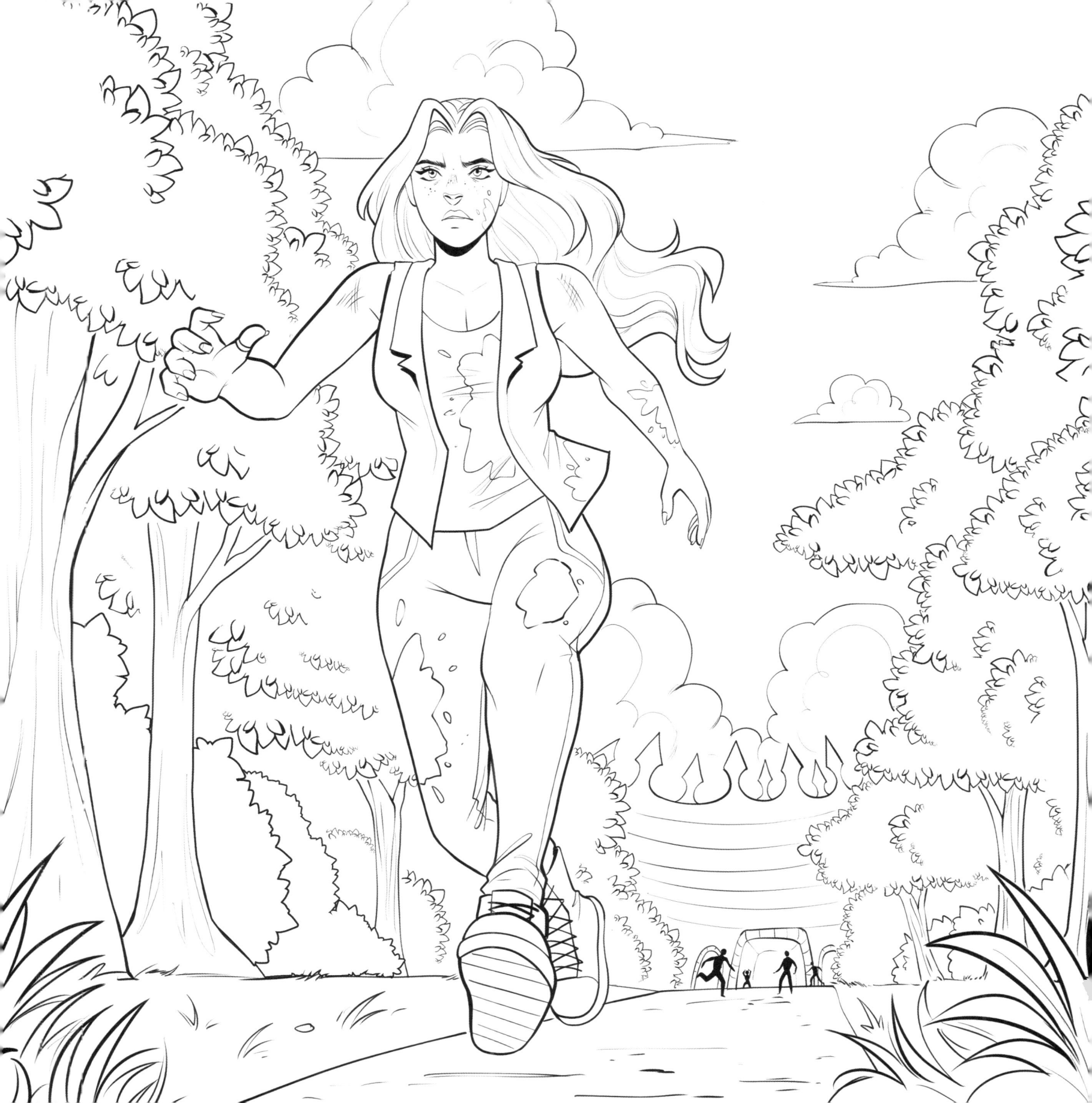

CALUM

STATUS: ELITE

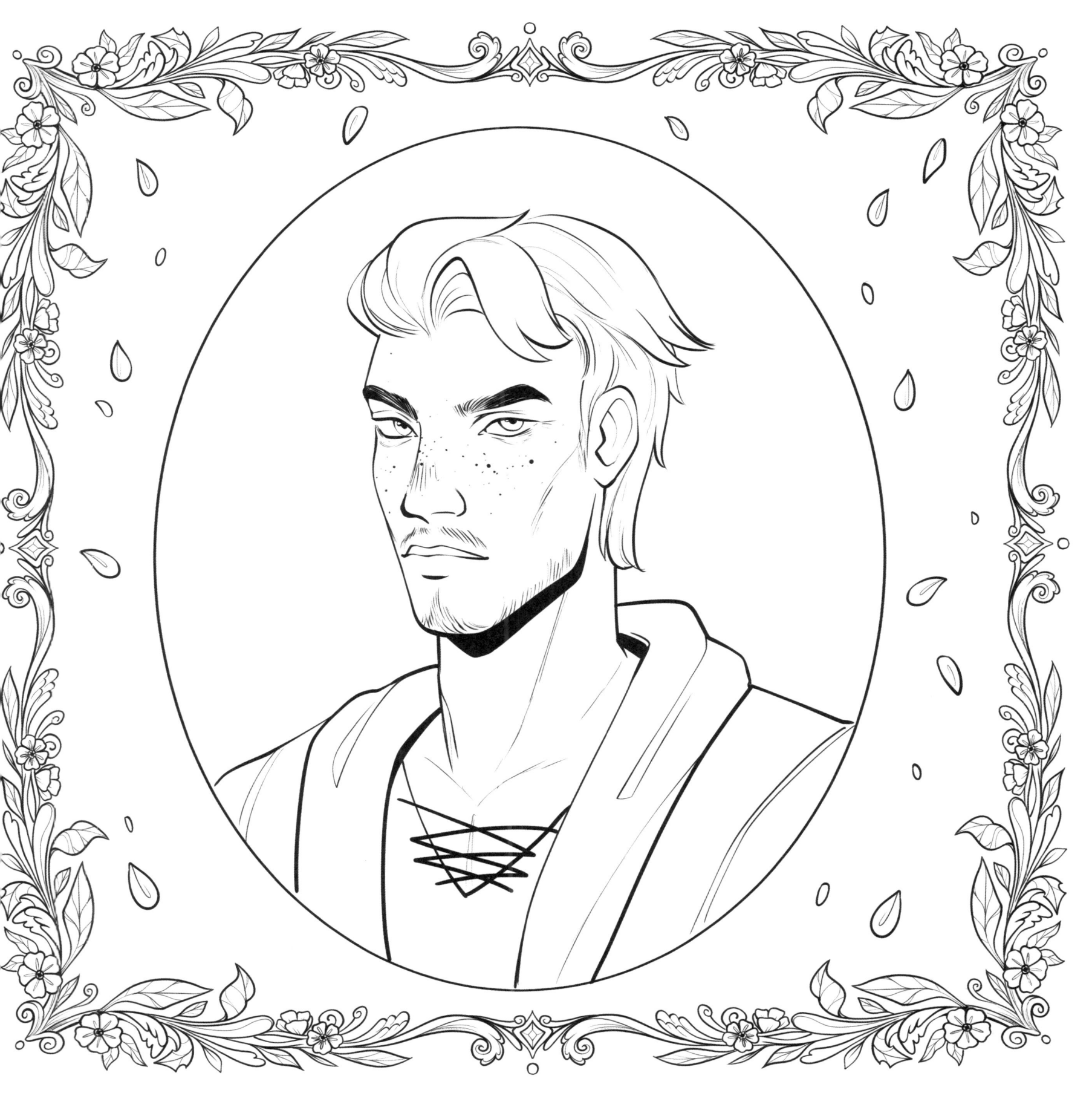

Not like this. I refuse to die like this.

"Is that all you care about?" My voice sounds foreign in my own ears, scratchy and scared. "Power? Ruling over an Elite kingdom? Does human life mean nothing to you?"

"Ordinaries are a weak excuse for life. An embarrassment," he growls. "They should have died with the Plague but instead they plague us."

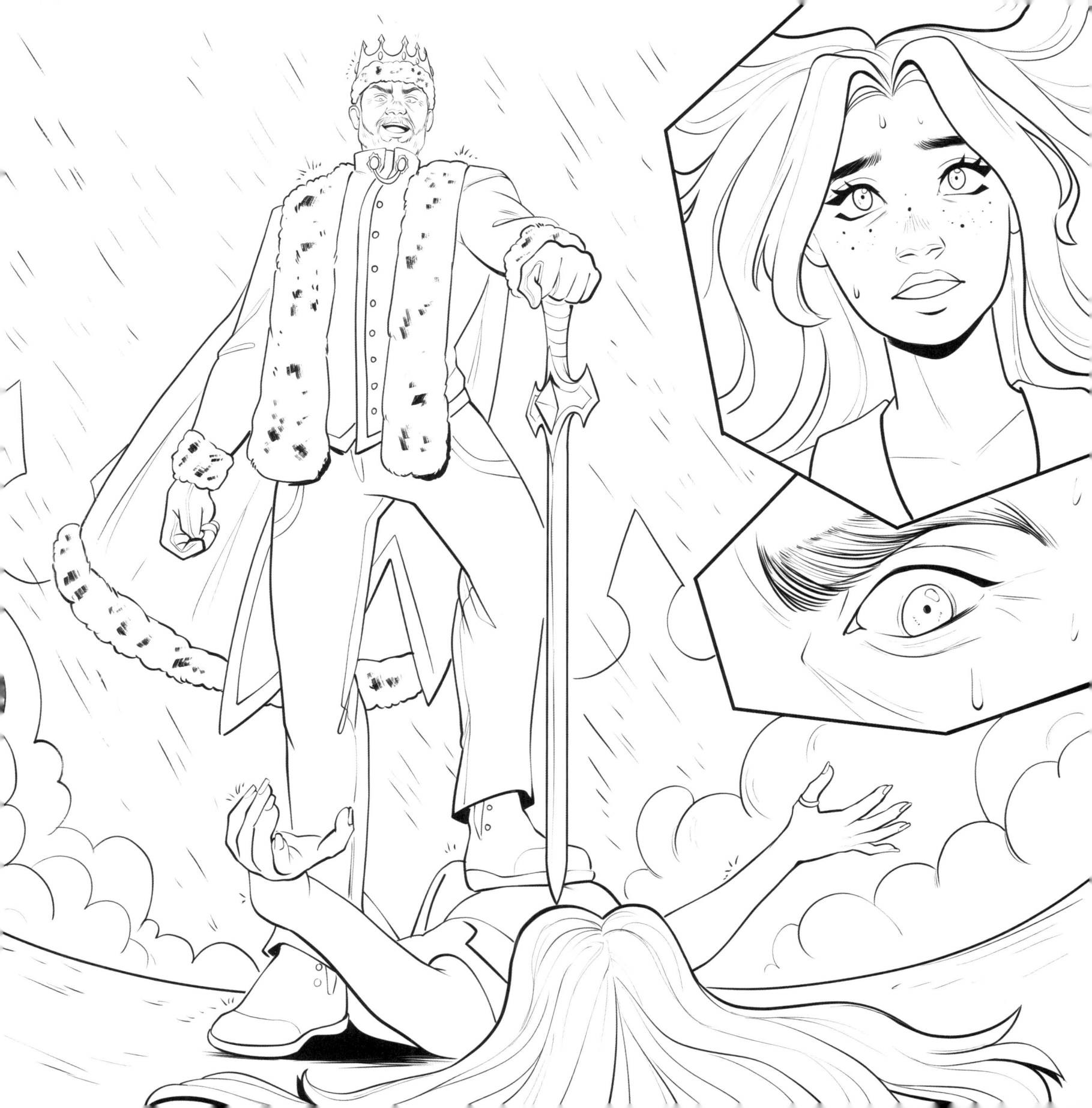

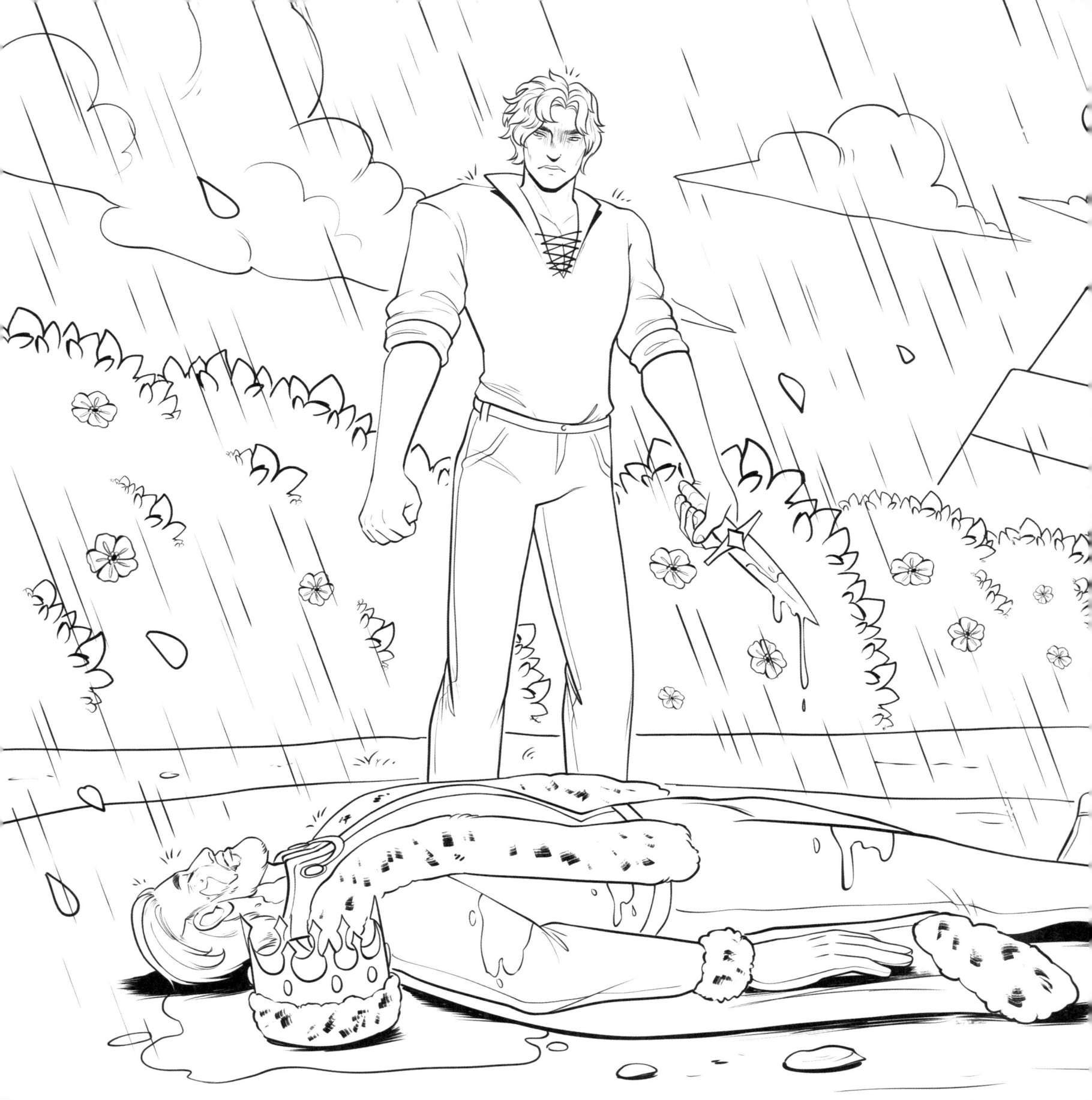

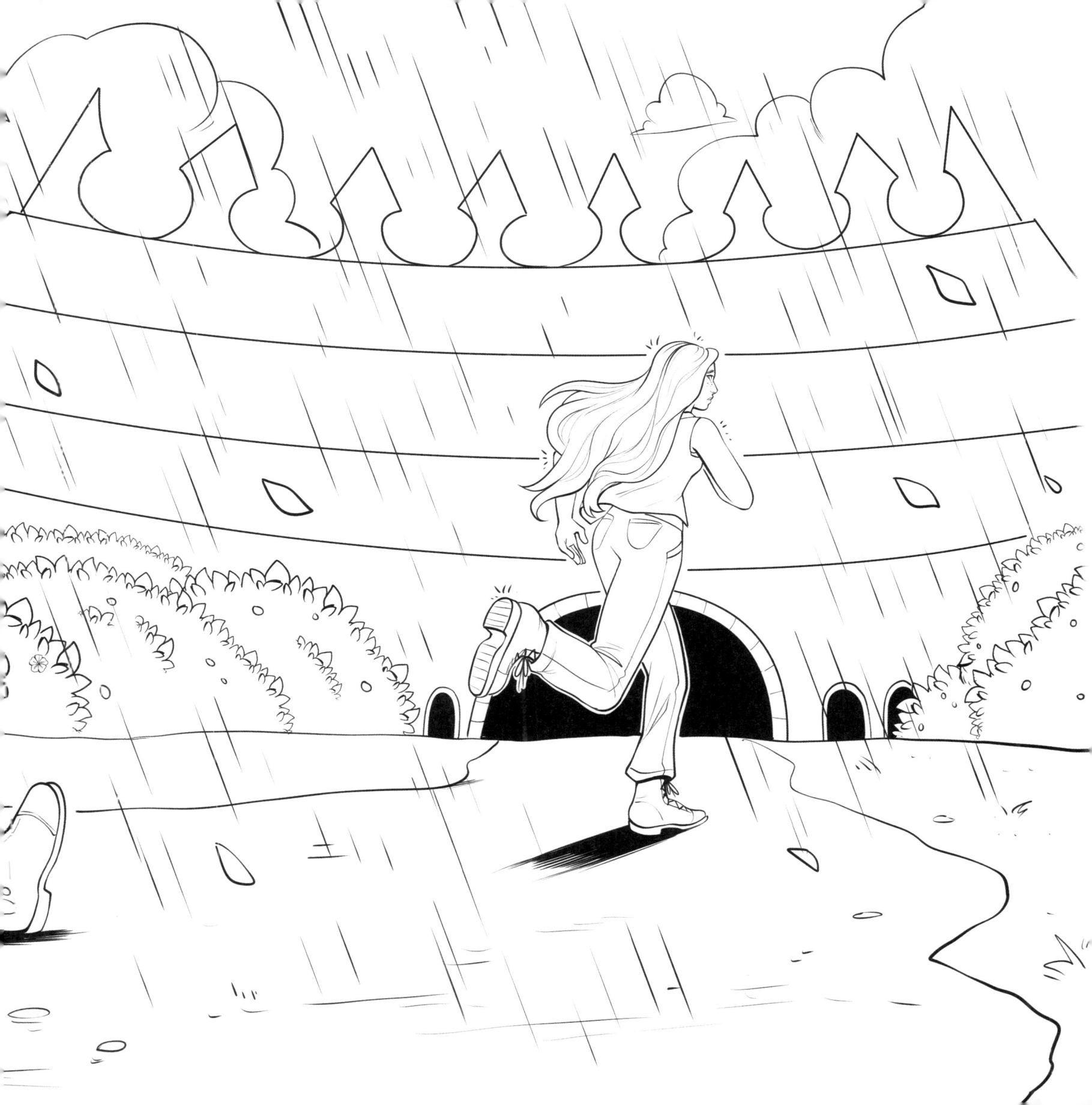

I knew I would be ruling over my brother one day. I just didn't think that day would come so soon, so suddenly.

I school my features into neutrality. "Find her."

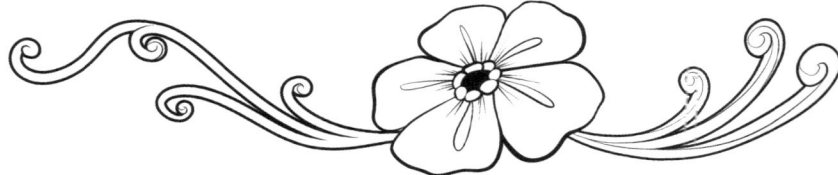

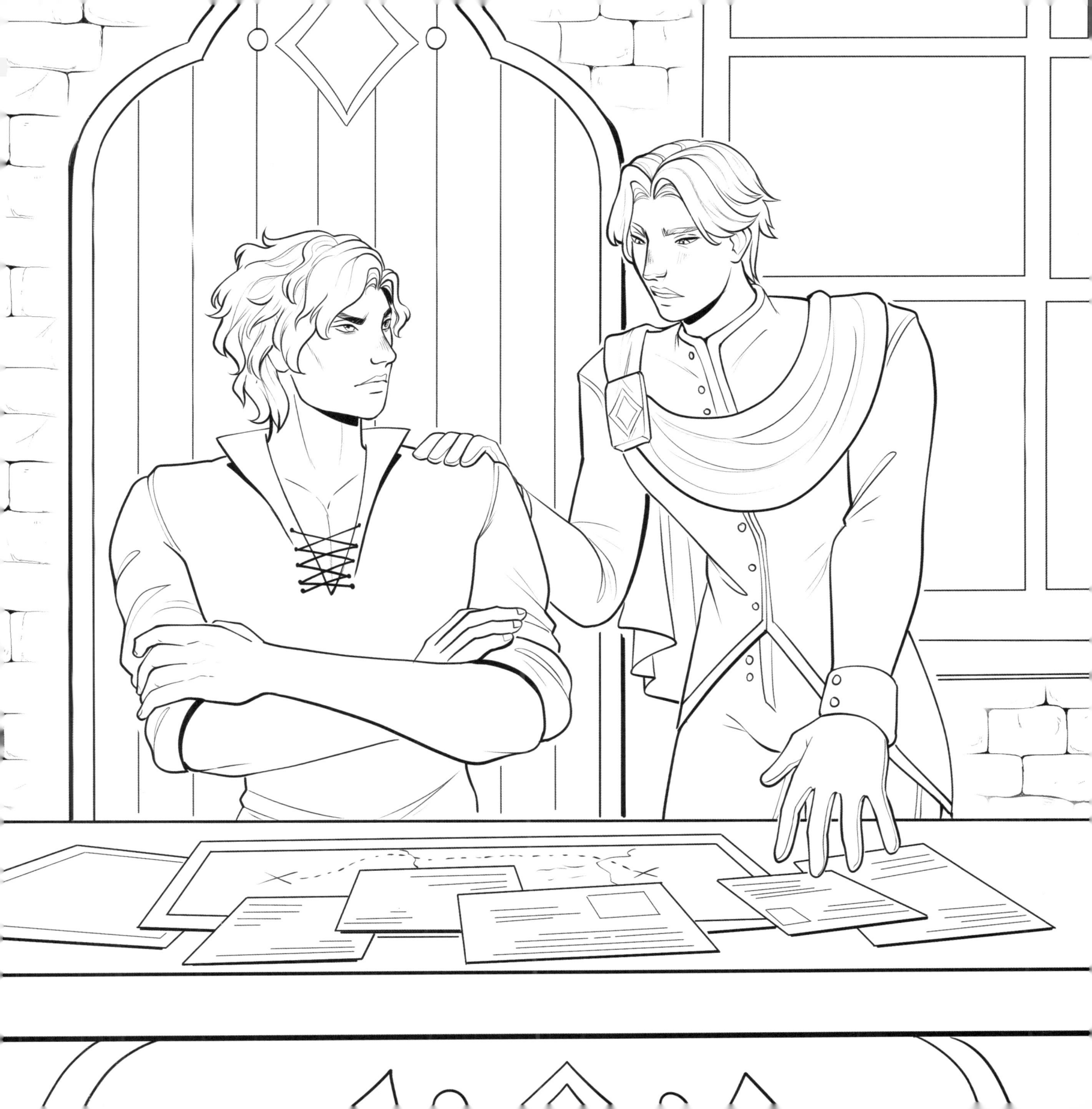

ABOUT THE AUTHOR

When Lauren Roberts isn't writing about fantasy worlds and bantering love interests, she can likely be found burrowed in bed reading about them. Lauren has lived in Michigan her whole life, making her very familiar with potholes, snow, and various lake activities. She has the hobbies of both a grandmother and a child: knitting, laser tag, hammocking, word searches, and coloring. She's the author of the Powerless Trilogy, and she hopes to have the privilege of writing pretty words for the rest of her life. If you enjoy ranting, reading, and writing, Lauren can be found on both TikTok and Instagram @laurenrobertslibrary or her website laurenrobertslibrary.com for your entertainment.

ABOUT THE ILLUSTRATOR

Alex comes from a family of creatives, their digital art career beginning at ten years old with a hand-me-down graphics tablet from their mum. Starting in the niche of fantasy and fandom with a penchant for painting, they now make a living drawing the things that bring them joy. When not working freelance, they can be found teaching Game Art and Illustration at a local university, or spending time with their beloved partner and two cats, Percy and Leela.